THE
EVERYDAY
AIRFRYER
COOKBOOK

THE EVERYDAY AIRFRYER COOKBOOK

Easy meals for one, two and more!

BEVERLEY JARVIS

Penguin Random House UK

To my sons Iain and Adam Piper.

If Adam hadn't introduced me to air fryers,

this book may never have happened.

CONTENTS

INTRODUCTION

When I purchased my first air fryer in 2021, I was determined to find a really useful cookbook, but sadly drew a blank and had to go online for recipes. This is the book I would have found invaluable when just starting out with my air fryer – an easy-to-use cookbook filled with inspiring, mostly healthy recipes that are great for everyday dishes and suitable for couples, families and those living alone, as well as including helpful information about air–frying.

An air fryer is an incredible appliance that allows you to cook a wide variety of dishes with very little, if any, added oil. While its name might lead some to perceive it to be a sort of deep-fat fryer, it is a small, yet high-powered convection oven. Air-fryers are speedy and economical to use, versatile, quick to reach temperature, easy to clean and consistently produce delicious food. You can use your air fryer to bake a pie, roast vegetables, cook a chicken, fry Scotch eggs, roast lamb, bake a cake and brown a shepherd's pie to perfection. You can even boil eggs for breakfast in it!

HOW TO USE AN AIR FRYER

There are two types of air fryers:

Basket air fryers are cylindrical in shape, containing one, or sometimes two, pull-out drawers, normally with a removable basket with holes. These are compact machines, available in various sizes and colours.

Oven-type air fryers are much heavier, larger machines and are similar in design to a toaster oven, but more cumbersome. It's not the sort of appliance to keep in storage, so you need space on a worktop for them permanently. They incorporate several functions and usually include a rotisserie attachment.

The recipes in this book are created for basket air fryers. There are currently many different makes, sizes and types of these available. Cooking timings vary slightly according to the size and electrical output of the machine, so you may need a minute or so less, or more, than times given. As soon as you open the drawer, the cooking stops. It restarts immediately after you re-insert the drawer, continuing to use the programme you have already set and without you needing to touch the controls.

Air fryers are wonderfully versatile appliances and can be used for a variety of purposes.

Reheating is quick and successful with delicious crisp results, unlike the microwave, which does not keep the food crisp when reheating.

When cooking a ready meal from frozen, timings will vary according to the type and size of ready meal as well as the output of your air fryer. If the meal container is suitable for domestic ovens, it will be suitable to place in an air fryer, too. Make sure the container fits into the basket before you start, taking care to remove and discard any film. You may want to cover the dish with foil, then remove this towards the end of reheating for a crispy top. Reheating times in an air fryer will be about 65 per cent of the time given on the container – I like to select a slightly lower temperature than suggested, too. Heat until the food is piping hot in the centre – you can use a cook's thermometer to test.

The air fryer can be plugged into any 13-amp socket and requires at least 13cm of space above and around the appliance, to allow for sufficient air flow. These mini convection ovens rely on a powerful electric element plus a constant flow of air, generated by a strong fan, to move the hot air around the food. The heat they generate is concentrated, cooking food quicker than conventional ovens.

An air fryer is also a very energy efficient choice for the kitchen. The machine I use has a capacity of 5.7 litres, with a maximum output of 1,700 watts, and weight of 5.95kg – normal domestic cookers have an output of 3,000 watts to 5,000 watts. On average, cooking food in an air fryer is 20 per cent faster, at temperatures about 15 per cent lower and can save considerably on energy costs, when used instead of your normal cooker. It usually takes about three minutes to pre-heat an air fryer, which also saves energy.

The air fryer is also fantastic for those who want to eat more healthily. It has a unique fat-removal technology – the tornado action of hot air removes excess fat while cooking your food beautifully. Any resulting fat is collected in the base of the drawer for easy disposal later.

Before cleaning your air fryer, always unplug the machine. As you've been cooking with little or no added oil, the surrounding area of your kitchen should remain clean, with no greasy splatters over the worktop. Cleaning the air fryer itself is easy; either wash the drawer and the removable basket and its base in hot soapy water in the sink, or pop them into the dishwasher if the manufacturer's instructions say it is safe to do so. You should wipe out the interior of the machine about once a week with a hot soapy cloth, then rinse well. The element needs occasional attention – wash with a soft brush and hot soapy water, then wipe clean. To remove stubborn stains and grease from inside the air fryer, make a thick paste from bicarbonate of soda and warm water. Spread over the affected area and leave to dry for a few hours or, preferably, overnight. Wipe off with a clean, hot, damp cloth. A friend of mine has even bought her air fryer its very own toothbrush, to occasionally clean the element! I find that, providing I wipe the cold element with a hot soapy cloth and then rinse well at least once a week, it hardly ever needs further attention.

ACCESSORIES FOR THE AIR FRYER

There is a good selection of useful accessories that are specifically designed for air fryers, all of which are readily available from stockists and online.

BAKING TINS

Baking tins specifically designed for air fryers, often with a heatproof handle, are useful for many recipes, such as the Flapjacks on page 50 and the Apple cake on page 179. However, you can also use any available solid ovenproof dish, providing it fits into the basket and allows air to circulate. Silicone muffin cases and cake containers are also available in various sizes, as are soufflé dishes and ramekins. The muffin cases and ramekins are ideal for cooking both muffins and small cakes, for frying and poaching eggs and for cooking Yorkshire puddings and filo pastry tarts.

TIN FOIL

Tin foil can be used in most models of air fryer. Check that your manufacturer endorses the use of foil and never allow tin foil to touch the element – make sure the foil is secured firmly to the cooking container when using it as a lid, to prevent it blowing around. Foil can also be used successfully to wrap foods and cook them in a parcel – such as the recipe for Stuffed sea bass on page 127.

REMOVEABLE LINER TRAYS

Some manufacturers provide a useful non-stick, perforated heatproof tray with a handle. This fits into base of the air fryer drawer and should be used for most foods, such as chips, jacket potatoes and sausages. It elevates the food slightly, helping air to circulate under and around it so it can cook to crisp perfection.

It can also be used to dehydrate fruit and vegetables and to bake snacks, chicken wings, etc. Easy to clean, I find these trays very useful. Those who own air fryers with these metal liner trays will seldom need to use parchment and silicone liners.

PERFORATED PARCHMENT AND SILICONE LINERS

To make life easier, use liners in your air fryer basket. They help to keep the basket clean and prevent food from sticking. These liners are perforated, allowing the hot air to circulate freely, and are just about the right size to fit the basket. They are useful for cooking all sorts of foods – particularly the silicone ones, which are mostly dishwasher safe and can be reused many times.

Never put baking parchment in the air fryer on its own as it will simply blow around at high speed and could become attached to the element, burning very quickly! Plastic containers, absorbent kitchen paper or wax paper are also no-nos. Plastic melts, and any wax coating will smoke and melt quickly, creating an awful mess to clear up! Absorbent kitchen paper will burn very quickly and could even catch fire.

METAL RACKS

Particularly useful when grilling foods, these good quality, stainless-steel metal racks are useful and widely available, but they are by no means vital. Food can be stacked on them to ensure proper air flow, and it also means you can cook more food at one time.

GRILL PAN

Useful, but not vital, the non-stick, pierced and ridged grill pans are designed specifically to be used in some air fryers as an attachment. Follow the instructions provided by the manufacturer. These pans are normally speedily pre-heated to a temperature of about 200°C in the air fryer, then used to sear and cook foods such as steak, fish and vegetables using just a little oil, to crisp perfection. Thanks to their superior non-stick surface, the grill pans are easy to clean, and most are dishwasher safe.

PIZZAS AND PIZZA ACCESSORIES

A pizza accessory is available from some manufacturers and can be used to bake your favourite pizza to perfect crispness. If no pizza accessory is available, heat or cook the prepared pizza directly in the basket or air fryer drawer using your crisper disc, if available.

COOKING TECHNIQUES IN THE AIR FRYER

There are a few new things to understand, and try to remember, as you master the exciting art of air frying.

BATCH COOKING

Batch cooking, in smaller amounts is speedy and more successful than overloading the basket with a large amount of food. Small air fryers cook food a little quicker than their bigger siblings, and batch cooking is particularly useful if you have a small air fryer and want to cook for a group of people. Don't worry about the first batch getting cold, as the food can be returned to the fryer, along with the second, cooked batch, for a minute or so to speedily reheat while you serve up the rest of the meal.

SHAKING OR TURNING FOOD

Shaking or turning food during cooking is frequently advised as it helps to ensure even cooking; follow the instructions given in each recipe. For those with arthritis, or other problems with their hands and who find this tricky, it is just as effective to gently toss or turn the food using a fish slice, kitchen tongs or similar rather than shaking the basket. Have a heatproof board beside your air fryer, ready to stand hot drawer on as you remove it from the appliance during cooking.

USING A FOIL SLING

If you are placing an accessory without a handle, such as a baking tin, into your air fryer basket it can often be a bit tricky to remove when hot. I like to construct a foil sling to act as a support, with handles, to fit under and around container and to remove it safely. To make your own foil sling, fold a piece of foil about 45cm long into a sturdy strip, about 5cm wide. You can reuse the strip of foil a few times before you need to replace it.

USEFUL INGREDIENTS

A word about some of the very handy ingredients, which I use frequently, for ease and speed, throughout the book

OIL SPRAY

A little oil spray is useful for many air fryer recipes. Dependent on the amount of food you are cooking, often just 5 sprays is enough, approximately 2 teaspoons. Avoid commercially produced oil sprays containing lecithin (you will see this mentioned in the list of ingredients) as it sticks to the inside of the air fryer and can be difficult to remove. For both convenience and economy, make up your own using a combination of approximately 70 per cent sunflower or rapeseed oil and 30 per cent light olive oil (sunflower and rapeseed oil crisp food better than olive oil). Store it in a spray bottle at an ambient temperature – I bought my spray bottle from the local garden centre.

GARLIC, CHILLI AND GINGER

For ease, speed and convenience, I sometimes like to use jars of ready-chopped garlic, chilli and ginger, available in most supermarkets. Once opened, the jars will keep, sealed, in the fridge for 5 weeks.

For reference:

1 tsp chopped ginger is the equivalent of 1 thumb-sized piece of fresh ginger

1 tsp chopped chilli is the equivalent of 1 large red chilli

1 tsp chopped garlic is the equivalent of 1 garlic clove

ONIONS

I like to use red onions, which are a little milder and sweeter than white. However, the choice, of course, is yours.

CURRY PASTE

Ready-made jars of curry paste in various flavours are also easy to find. Curry paste keeps in the fridge once opened, sealed, for up to 6 weeks.

HERBS

I like to use fresh herbs when possible. But for ease and speed, both dried and frozen herbs are great convenience items.

BLACK PEPPER

I often like to use freshly ground black pepper in my recipes. It is a valuable source of vitamins B, C and K, as well as many important minerals, including potassium.

GETTING STARTED

TOAST

While toasters are great for cooking sliced bread, the air fryer works particularly well when preparing tea cakes, burger buns, waffles or even crumpets.

Serves 1

Accessories (optional)
Metal rack

Ingredients
2 slices of bread or 1 tea cake sliced
   in half

1. Heat the air fryer to 200°C.

2. Arrange the bread slices or tea cake halves in the air fryer basket. Air-fry for 3 minutes, then flip and cook for 1–2 minutes more on the other side, or until golden.

3. To cook more toast at one time, use a metal rack.

BACK BACON

Serves 1

Ingredients

2 rashers back bacon

1. Heat the air fryer to 200°C.

2. Arrange the bacon rashers in the base of the air–fryer basket. Air-fry for 3–4 minutes. Flip the bacon, using tongs, and continue to air-fry for a further 1–2 minutes, or until cooked to your liking.

TIP:
When cooking 4 rashers at once, air-fry for 5 minutes, flip and continue to air-fry for 2 minutes.

GARLIC AND HERB CIABATTA

I like to use a metal rack to cook my garlic bread in the air fryer, especially when I'm catering for the family.

Serves 4

Accessories (optional)
Metal rack

Ingredients
1½ tbsp olive oil
2 tsp chopped fresh coriander
1 garlic clove, crushed
2 ciabatta rolls
Salt and ground black pepper

1. Heat the air fryer to 190°C.

2. In a mixing bowl, combine the olive oil, coriander and garlic. Season with salt and pepper.

3. Cut each ciabatta roll in half, then half again, to give you 8 pieces. Using a pastry brush, spread the flavoured oil over the bread and arrange in the air fryer basket.

4. Air-fry for approximately 4 minutes. If using a rack, remove the top layer of bread when golden. Remove the rack and continue to cook the lower layer for a further minute until golden too. If you don't have a rack, cook the ciabatta slices 4 at a time.

TIP:

For a cheesy version, divide about 40g grated Cheddar or Parmesan cheese evenly between the pieces of ciabatta, and return the bread to the air fryer, for a further minute or so, at 190°C, after first cooking, until crisp and golden.

BAKED POTATO

Serves 1

Accessories

Baking dish suitable for microwave and air fryer

Ingredients

1 medium baking potato
Oil spray
Salt and ground black pepper

1. Heat the air fryer to 200°C.

2. Wash and dry the potato. Mark a deep cross in the top of the potato using a sharp vegetable knife, then lightly spray with oil.

3. Season with salt and pepper and arrange in the baking dish. Microwave on full power for 4 minutes.

4. Transfer the dish to the air fryer basket and air-fry for approximately 30 minutes, turning the potato over after 12 minutes, until the skin is crisp and golden, and the potato is cooked through.

TIP:

If you don't have a microwave, simply air-fry the prepared potato, or potatoes, for about 50 minutes at 200°C.

If cooking 2, 3 or 4 potatoes air fryer cooking time remains the same. However, microwave cooking times will vary. For 2 potatoes microwave for 7 minutes, before cooking in the air–fryer. For 3 potatoes, microwave for 12 minutes and for 4 potatoes, microwave for 14 minutes.

MARINATED LAMB CHOPS

Serves 2

Ingredients

Juice of ½ lime
1 tbsp olive oil
Handful fresh coriander, chopped
½ garlic clove, chopped
4 small lamb chops
Oil spray
Salt and ground black pepper

1. To make the marinade, add the lime juice, olive oil, coriander and garlic to a mixing bowl and season with salt and pepper. Stir to combine.

2. Arrange the lamb chops in a shallow dish, pour the marinade over and set aside for 10–15 minutes.

3. Heat the air fryer to 190°C.

4. Lightly spray the air fryer basket with a little oil before lifting the chops from the marinade and placing them in the basket. Air-fry for 7 minutes before removing the basket and turning the chops over. Increase the temperature to 200°C and continue to air-fry the chops for 2 minutes, or until cooked to your liking.

CHICKEN BREASTS

Serves 2

Ingredients
2 chicken breast fillets
Oil spray
½ tsp dried mixed herbs
Salt and ground black pepper

1. Heat the air fryer to 180°C.

2. Lightly spray the top of each chicken breast with a little oil and sprinkle with the dried herbs and a light seasoning of salt and pepper. Coat the basket with a little oil spray before arranging the chicken breasts in the air fryer basket.

3. Air-fry for 10–13 minutes, then leave in the air fryer with the machine switched off and the drawer closed for 3 minutes.

4. Remove from the basket and check the chicken is fully cooked by piercing the thickest part of the breast with a sharp knife. If cooked, the juices will run clear. If it is not yet cooked, return to the air fryer for a further minute, or until cooked.

PORK SAUSAGES

Serves 2

Ingredients

4 pork sausages, straight from
the fridge

1. Heat the air fryer to 190°C.

2. Arrange the sausages in the air fryer basket.
   Air-fry for 5–9 minutes, removing and shaking
   the basket after 3 minutes, until cooked
   and browned.

BASMATI RICE

While it may be quicker to cook rice in a covered pan on the hob, this foolproof method produces perfect fluffy rice every time.

Serves 2

Accessories
Baking accessory tin, approx. 18cm square x 8cm deep, or a large soufflé dish

Ingredients
150ml white basmati rice
300ml boiling water
Pinch of salt

1. Heat the air fryer to 180°C.

2. Rinse the rice in a sieve under cold running water. Drain well, then place in an air fryer baking accessory tin, or similar container, which fits into your air fryer basket, allowing a little space all round the container.

3. Pour over the boiling water, add the salt, and cover the container tightly with tin foil, then air-fry for 20 minutes. Remove the container from the air fryer and let the rice stand, covered, for about 3 minutes.

4. Remove the foil, fluff up the rice with a fork and serve.

TIP:

For speed and easy measuring, I use the same 300ml breakfast mug to measure both the rice and the boiling water. Alternatively use a measuring jug.

If you wish to double the recipe, simply double both the amount of rice and boiling water. Use the same cooking container, as directed. Add a pinch of salt and cover with foil. Air-fry at 180°C for 30 minutes. Continue as given for 2 servings.

FROZEN FISH FINGERS

Serves 2

Accessories (optional)
Metal rack

Ingredients
Oil spray
6 frozen fish fingers

1. Heat the air fryer to 190°C.

2. Lightly spray the air fryer basket with a little oil or use a lightly oiled liner. Arrange the fish fingers in the basket. Spray with a little oil. Air-fry for 9–11 minutes, turning the fish fingers after 6 minutes. They are ready when the crumb is crisp, and the centres of the fish fingers are piping hot.

3. Transfer to a plate lined with absorbent kitchen paper, then serve.

TIP:

Frozen breaded products, such as fish fingers, mushrooms, scampi, etc, can be cooked without the addition of added oil. However, I prefer to add just a couple of sprays of oil when cooking these products.

FROZEN BREADED GARLIC MUSHROOMS

Serves 2

Ingredients
8 frozen breaded garlic
   mushrooms
Oil spray

1. Heat the air fryer to 200°C

2. Lightly spray the air fryer basket with a little oil, before arranging the mushrooms in the air fryer basket. Spray the mushrooms with a little oil.

3. Air-fry for 6–7 minutes, shaking or turning the mushrooms after 4 minutes. The mushrooms are ready when they are crisp and golden. These are delicious served with the Tartare sauce on page 32.

FROZEN BREADED SCAMPI WITH SPEEDY TARTARE SAUCE

Serves 2

Ingredients
Oil spray
180g frozen scampi

For the tartare sauce
150ml mayonnaise, shop bought or
   use the recipe on p101
2 tbsp capers, drained and
   chopped
2 tbsp gherkins, drained and
   chopped
Squeeze of fresh lemon juice
Handful of fresh parsley, chopped
Salt and ground black pepper

1. Heat the air fryer to 200°C.

2. Lightly spray the air fryer basket with a little oil, before arranging the scampi in the basket and air-frying for 4 minutes. Remove the basket and gently shake or turn over the scampi. Continue to air-fry for a further 3 minutes, until crisp and golden.

3. To make the tartare sauce, add the mayonnaise, capers, gherkins, lemon juice and parsley into a bowl. Season with a little salt and pepper and stir to combine before serving with the scampi.

4. The sauce can be stored in an airtight container in the fridge for up to 4 days.

FROZEN SWEET POTATO FRIES

Serves 2

Ingredients
450g frozen sweet potato fries

1. Heat the air fryer to 190°C.

2. Place the sweet potato fries into the air fryer basket and air-fry for 5 minutes. Remove and shake the basket, then air-fry for a further 5–10 minutes, until crisp, golden and cooked to your liking.

3. Shake again, then serve.

FROZEN CRINKLE CUT CHIPS

Serves 2

Ingredients
450g frozen
crinkle cut chips

1. Heat the air fryer to 200°C.

2. Place the chips in the air fryer basket. Air-fry for 5 minutes. Remove and shake the basket, then air-fry for 10–15 minutes, shaking now and then, until crisp, golden and cooked to your liking. Cooking the chips for longer will mean they are crispier.

3. Shake, then serve.

SPEEDY ROASTIES

Serves 2

Ingredients

450g potatoes (I like to use a mixture of sweet and white, Maris Piper, white potatoes, if possible)

1 tsp semolina (alternatively use cornflour or polenta)

Oil spray

Sea salt

1. Peel and cut the potatoes into chunks, then simmer on the hob in a covered pan of boiling water for 11 minutes.

2. Heat the air fryer to 200°C

3. Drain the potatoes well, then shake the pan to roughen the edges. Sprinkle over the semolina and add 10 sprays of oil. Toss together, then turn into the air fryer basket.

4. Air-fry for 20–25 minutes, shaking twice during cooking, until crisp and golden. Serve immediately, sprinkled with freshly ground sea salt.

ROAST HEADS OF GARLIC

Roast garlic cloves are delicious when used to add flavour to mashed potatoes, carrots or swede, or to give mayonnaise a kick. They can also be added to the tomato base on a pizza, to flavour butter for garlic bread and to liven up hummus.

Ingredients

Up to 4 heads of garlic

Oil spray

1. Heat the air fryer to 190°C.

2. Slice the tops off the garlic heads, to expose the cloves. Spray each head with a little oil and wrap each in a square of foil, bringing up the corners to meet at the top and enclose the garlic. Seal, place in the basket and air-fry for 25–30 minutes.

3. Remove the basket from the air fryer. Carefully unwrap the garlic (the foil will be very hot!) and use as required.

ROAST BUTTERNUT SQUASH RINGS

Serves 2

Ingredients

4 thick rings cut from a butternut
    squash, seeds removed

Oil spray

Salt and ground black pepper

1. Heat the air fryer to 180°C.

2. Lightly spray both sides of each of the rings with a little oil and season with salt and pepper. Spray the basket with a little oil before adding the squash rings, in a single layer, and air-frying for approximately 14 minutes.

3. Flip the rings over and continue to air-fry at 200°C for 2 minutes, until they are golden and tender in the centre when pierced with a sharp knife.

SUMMER HERBS

Ingredients

Sprigs of fresh rosemary, thyme
and mint
Kitchen string

1. Heat the air fryer to 180°C.

2. Tie the rosemary, thyme and mint sprigs into
3 separate small bundles with kitchen string,
to stop them flying around.

3. Air-fry for about 4 minutes, turning each bundle
over after 2 minutes.

4. Cool and crumble into an airtight container
for winter use.

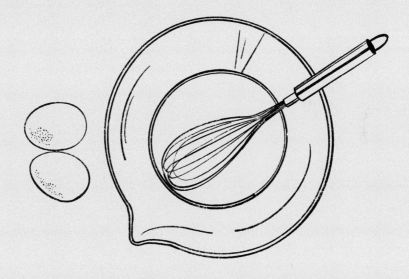

BREAKFAST
AND BRUNCH

FRITTATA WITH FETA AND PARMESAN

Frittata makes a delicious breakfast or light lunch that is popular with all. This recipe uses 2 types of cheese for extra flavour.

Serves 2

Accessories
Baking accessory tin or non-stick, solid-base cake tin (approx. 18cm square x 8cm deep)
Foil sling (see page 18)

Ingredients
Oil spray
4 large eggs
1 medium tomato, chopped
1 small red or green pepper, deseeded and chopped
½ tsp dried mixed herbs
40g feta cheese, crumbled
40g Parmesan cheese, grated
Salt and ground black pepper
Mixed salad, to serve

1. Heat the air fryer to 200°C. Lightly grease the base and sides of the tin with a little oil.

2. Add the tomato and bell pepper to the tin. Spray with a little oil and place the tin into the air fryer basket. Air-fry for 3 minutes. Stir, and set aside. Reduce the temperature of the air fryer to 170°C.

3. In a large mixing bowl, beat the eggs with 2 tablespoons of cold water using a balloon whisk or fork, until foaming. Stir the mixed herbs into the beaten egg with a light seasoning of salt and ground black pepper.

4. Pour the egg mixture into the tin and scatter the crumbled feta and Parmesan cheese evenly over the surface. Put the baking tin into the air fryer basket, using the strip of foil if there is no handle on your container (see page 18). Air-fry for 11–13 minutes or until the frittata is set in the middle and golden on top.

5. Carefully remove the tin from the air fryer. Set aside for a few minutes, then use a spatula or knife to run round the edge of the tin to loosen it and to help you upturn it onto a large plate.

6. Serve in wedges, with a mixed salad.

EGGS FOR ONE

Eggs are cheap to buy, super nutritious, quick to cook and popular with most people. It came as quite a revelation to me to realise that I could even boil eggs in my air fryer!

BOILED EGGS

You can cook up to 6 eggs at the same time. Cooking times remain as given.

Accessories (optional)
Metal rack

Ingredients
2 large eggs

1. Heat the air fryer to 120°C.

2. Take the eggs out of the fridge and put them carefully into the basket of your air-fryer, or use a metal rack, if available. Air-fry for 10 minutes for soft-boiled eggs, or for 14 minutes for hard-boiled eggs.

3. If preparing hard-boiled eggs, remove from the air fryer and plunge into a bowl of iced water. Once cool enough to handle, peel the eggs under the water for ease and speed.

FRIED EGGS

Accessories
2 pie dishes or ramekins

Ingredients
Oil spray, for greasing
2 large eggs

1. Heat the air fryer to 190°C.

2. Grease the pie dishes or ramekins. Crack 1 egg into each. Place in the air fryer basket and air-fry for 3–5 minutes, or until the eggs are fried to your liking.

3. Carefully remove them from the basket and, using a spatula, transfer to a plate.

SCRAMBLED EGGS

Ingredients
2 eggs
2 tbsp milk
Salt and ground black pepper

1. Heat the air fryer to 160°C.

2. In a medium mixing bowl, or Pyrex jug, suitable for use in the air fryer, whisk the eggs with the milk and season with salt and pepper. Place in the air fryer basket.

3. Air-fry for 3 minutes, then remove and beat gently, using a balloon whisk, before air-frying at 150°C for 3 minutes, or until the egg is scrambled to your liking.

4. Stir again and serve.

TIP:
When making scrambled eggs in the air fryer, using a jug with a handle makes life easier.

POACHED EGGS

Accessories
2 ramekins or large silicone muffin cases

Ingredients
Softened butter, for greasing
2 large eggs

1. Heat the air fryer to 200°C.

2. Grease the ramekins or large silicone muffin cases with a little soft butter. Place in the air fryer basket, then add 2 tablespoons of water to each container.

3. Air-fry for 3 minutes, until the water is boiling. Carefully open the drawer and crack 1 egg into each container.

4. Air-fry at 180°C for 5–6 minutes, or until the eggs are cooked to your liking.

5. Carefully remove from the drawer, using oven gloves, and use a spatula to serve the perfectly poached eggs.

SOLO ENGLISH BREAKFAST

Bacon, sausages, tomato and egg can all be cooked together for a speedy breakfast for one person.

Serves 1

Accessories
1 ramekin

Ingredients
Softened butter, for greasing
2 pork sausages
1 tomato, halved
2 rashers bacon
1 egg
1 slice of wholemeal toast, to serve
½ avocado, sliced, to serve (optional)

1. Heat the air fryer to 190°C. Grease the ramekin with softened butter.

2. Place the sausages in the air fryer basket and cook for 4 minutes. Shake the basket, then add the tomato and bacon, then crack the egg into the greased ramekin. Add to the basket and air-fry for a further 4-5 minutes, until the bacon and egg are cooked to your liking.

3. Serve with freshly made wholemeal toast and sliced avocado.

BACON WITH MUSHROOMS

This makes a quick and easy breakfast. I like to serve it with chunks of sourdough bread and a mixed salad. You can halve this recipe, to serve 1 person. Allow approximately 5 minutes of cooking time, if halving.

Serves 2

Ingredients
100g button mushrooms, sliced
Oil spray
4 rashers back bacon, rind removed
Mixed salad or sliced avocado,
    to serve

1. Heat the air fryer to 200°C.

2. Arrange the mushrooms in the basket, evenly spread out and spray with a little oil. Arrange the bacon rashers on top of the mushrooms. Air-fry for 6–9 minutes, flipping the bacon after 5 minutes, until cooked to your liking.

3. Serve immediately, accompanied by a salad or slices of avocado.

GOAT'S CHEESE AND PARSLEY OMELETTE

This tasty omelette makes a filling breakfast or lunch for one person and is simply delicious served with salad or baked beans.

Serves 1

Accessories
Baking accessory tin or non-stick, solid-base cake tin (approx. 18cm square x 8cm deep)
Foil sling (see page 18)

Ingredients
3 medium eggs
15g butter
1 tbsp chopped fresh parsley
2 spring onions, chopped (optional)
75g goat's cheese, roughly chopped, or 50g mature Cheddar cheese, grated
Salt and ground black pepper
Sliced tomatoes, to serve

1. Heat the air fryer to 190°C.

2. In a medium mixing bowl and using a balloon whisk, beat the eggs with 2 tablespoons of water, until foaming. Season with salt and pepper.

3. Put the butter into the tin, then place the tin in the air fryer basket and air-fry for 1–2 minutes, until melted and hot. Stir in the parsley and spring onions, if using, and continue to air-fry for 1 minute.

4. Pour the beaten eggs into the tin, sprinkle over the cheese evenly, then air-fry at 170°C for 11–13 minutes, until well risen, golden and cooked in the middle.

5. Carefully remove from the air fryer and use a spatula or knife to run around the edge of the omelette to loosen it from the tin. Transfer to a serving platter and serve with sliced tomatoes.

SAVOURY CHEESE AND CARROT FLAPJACKS

These tasty, light, savoury flapjacks make a great and nutritious breakfast item. A delicious recipe that you will come back to again and again.

Makes 8–10 flapjacks

Accessories

Baking accessory tin or non-stick, solid-base cake tin (approx. 18cm square x 8cm deep)

Foil sling (see page 18)

Ingredients

25g butter

1 tbsp olive oil

125g porridge oats

1 carrot, grated

75g mature Cheddar cheese, grated

2 large eggs, beaten

1 tbsp sunflower or pumpkin seeds

Salt and ground black pepper

1. Heat the air fryer to 190°C.

2. Heat the butter in the tin in the air fryer basket for about 2 minutes, until melted. Carefully remove the tin from the air fryer and, using a pastry brush, grease the base and sides of the tin with the melted butter.

3. Tip the remaining butter into a large mixing bowl and add the olive oil, oats, grated carrot, cheese, eggs, seeds and some salt and pepper. Mix with a fork to ensure everything is well combined. Tip the mixture into the prepared tin and press down firmly and evenly, all over, using the back of the fork.

4. Transfer the tin to the air fryer basket and air-fry for approximately 12–15 minutes, until the top is golden and sizzling. Remove from the basket and set aside for about 15 minutes.

5. Turn out onto a chopping board and cut into 8–10 pieces while still warm. Delicious served warm, but these will also store well in the fridge or a cool larder, in an airtight container, for up to 2 days.

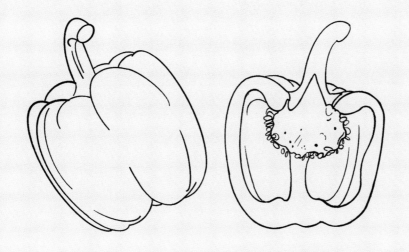

LIGHT
LUNCHES

BAKED SWEET POTATO WITH AVOCADO, SWEETCORN AND SPRING ONIONS

I like to serve this with a spinach, red pepper, sweetcorn and chopped tomato salad, tossed with a lemon juice and olive oil vinaigrette, flavoured with sea salt, Dijon mustard and a touch of honey. If cooking 2, 3 or 4 sweet potatoes, the cooking time remains the same.

Serves 1

Ingredients
1 medium sweet potato
1 tsp olive oil
Salad, to serve (see intro)

For the filling
2 red or white spring onions, chopped
¼ x 160g tin sweetcorn kernels, drained
¼ red pepper, deseeded and finely chopped
½ medium ripe avocado, stoned and diced
½ tsp lemon juice
1 tbsp crème fraîche
½ tbsp grated Cheddar or Emmental cheese (optional)
Salt and ground black pepper

1. Heat the air fryer to 190°C.

2. Scrub the potato, then blot dry in between sheets of absorbent kitchen paper, then place on a chopping board and prod all over with a fork.

3. Brush the potato with the oil and season with salt and pepper. Place in the air fryer basket and air-fry for 45 minutes, turning over after 20 minutes, until the potato is cooked right through and the skin is crisp.

4. Meanwhile, prepare the filling. In a medium mixing bowl, combine the spring onions, sweetcorn, red pepper, avocado, lemon juice and crème fraîche. Season with salt and pepper and mix gently, just to combine.

5. Remove the potato from the air fryer basket and stand it on a chopping board. Slit the potato open and add the filling. Top with the grated cheese, if using, and serve immediately, accompanied by the salad (see intro).

CHEESE AND TOMATO BREAD ROLL TOASTIES

I developed this recipe when I had a day-old bread roll left in the larder that needed using up. It was so delicious I thought I would share it here. To serve 2, simply double the ingredients and cook both rolls together for 7–8 minutes, flipping after 5 minutes.

Serves 1

Ingredients

1 wholemeal bread roll

A little softened butter, for spreading

1 ½ Cheddar cheese slices or 40g Cheddar cheese, grated

1 tomato, half of it sliced

½ tbsp olive oil

½ tsp dried mixed herbs

A little freshly grated Parmesan cheese

Salt and ground black pepper

1. Heat the air fryer to 190°C.

2. For easy handling, cut the roll in half horizontally, but do not cut right through. Butter very lightly. Add the cheese slices, or the grated Cheddar. Top the cheese with a few slices of tomato. Season with a little salt and pepper.

3. Close the roll, to enclose the filling completely. In a small mug, combine the olive oil and herbs. Using a pastry brush, brush the herby oil over the outside of the roll and the remaining tomato half.

4. Place the roll in the air fryer basket and add the tomato half. Air-fry for 5-7 minutes, carefully flipping the roll after 3 minutes.

5. Remove the roll from the air fryer and scatter the Parmesan cheese over the top of the tomato half. Continue to cook the tomato half in the air fryer for a further 1–2 minutes at 200°C, until the cheese is melted and golden.

CHEESE AND PICKLE TOASTIES

My adult children and my grandchildren love these tasty toasties. I prefer to cook them in the air fryer now, rather than having to wash up the sandwich toaster after lunch! If you own a metal rack, you can air-fry 2 toasties at the same time – the cooking time will remain about the same.

Serves 1

Ingredients

2 slices of bread, preferably
    wholemeal, cut from a large loaf
A little softened butter, for
    spreading
1 tbsp sweet pickle, small chunks
    if possible
40g Cheddar cheese, grated
Oil spray
Coleslaw, to serve

1. Heat the air fryer to 180°C.

2. On a chopping board, lightly spread one side of each slice of bread with a little spread or softened butter.

3. Arrange one bread slice on the chopping board, buttered side down. Spread the pickle on the unbuttered side and top with the grated cheese, reserving a small amount to add to the top of the sandwich. Using a fish slice to help you, top with the second slice of bread, buttered side up.

4. Lightly spray the air fryer basket with a little oil. Cut the sandwich in half, then arrange in the base of the basket, ensuring the 2 half sandwiches are not touching. Sprinkle with the reserved cheese

5. Air-fry for 5–7 minutes, or until golden, and serve with coleslaw.

VEGGIE BURGERS WITH TOMATO AND RED PEPPER SALSA

These delicious veggie burgers make a great brunch or snack for 4 people, or the recipe can be halved to serve 2; the cooking time remains the same. Serve with the salsa or even the Curry sauce on page 79.

Serves 4

Ingredients
For the burgers
1 medium carrot (approx. 120g), grated
1 small sweet potato (approx. 80g), peeled and grated
1 garlic clove, crushed
½ tsp dried thyme
1 tbsp fresh basil leaves, torn
70g porridge oats
50g Cheddar cheese, grated
25g Parmesan cheese, grated
25g walnuts, chopped
1 large egg, beaten
Flour, for dusting
Oil spray
Salt and ground black pepper

For the salsa
3 medium tomatoes, chopped
2 spring onions (red are nice), chopped
½ red pepper, deseeded and diced
1 celery stick, chopped
1 tbsp chopped fresh coriander
1 tbsp chopped fresh mint or parsley
1 tsp lemon juice
1 tbsp pumpkin seeds (optional, but nice)

1. To make the burgers, combine the grated carrot, sweet potato, garlic, thyme, basil, oats, both types of cheese and the walnuts in a large mixing bowl. Stir well to combine. Add a light seasoning of salt and plenty of pepper. Add the egg and stir well, then cover and chill in the fridge for 15 minutes or up to 3 hours.

2. Heat the air fryer to 170°C.

3. Remove the bowl from the fridge and on a lightly floured chopping board, using damp hands, form the mixture into 4 flat burgers. Spray each burger on both sides with a little oil, and lightly spray the air fryer basket with oil before placing the burgers in the basket. Air-fry for 8 minutes, until golden brown and cooked through.

4. Meanwhile, make the salsa. Put all the ingredients for the salsa, except the pumpkin seeds, into a mixing bowl. Stir or toss well to combine. Add salt and pepper to taste. Stir again. Top with the pumpkin seeds, if using.

5. Serve the burgers with the freshly prepared salsa.

GRILLED AUBERGINE WITH YOGHURT DRESSING

Aubergine cooked in the air fryer is simply delicious and far healthier than frying the slices in copious amounts of oil. I like to serve this with the Sunday roast, or just on its own for lunch with scrambled eggs.

Serves 2

Ingredients

1 medium aubergine, sliced into rings
1–2 tbsp olive oil
Oil spray
Salt and ground black pepper

For the yoghurt dressing

150g natural Greek yoghurt
1 garlic clove, crushed
½ thumb-size piece of fresh ginger, grated
Grated zest and juice of ½ lemon
Small bunch of fresh mint leaves, roughly chopped, plus a few sprigs to serve
Pomegranate seeds, to serve

1. Put the aubergine slices into a colander and sprinkle liberally with salt. Top with a plate and a weight and set aside for 20 minutes. This helps to draw moisture out of the aubergine, which will crisp up better if you do this.

2. Heat the air fryer to 200°C.

3. Do not rinse the aubergine, but blot the slices dry between sheets of absorbent kitchen paper, knocking off most of the salt. Drizzle, brush or spray the aubergine slices on both sides with a little olive oil.

4. Add the aubergine slices to the air fryer basket and cook for about 15 minutes, flipping, using tongs or a fish slice, halfway through, and spraying with a little more oil. Continue to cook until charred and soft.

5. Meanwhile, make the dressing. In a medium mixing bowl, combine the yoghurt, garlic, ginger, lemon zest and juice and chopped mint. Stir in salt and pepper to taste, then turn into a serving dish.

6. Serve the aubergine with the pomegranate seeds, sprinkled with a few tiny sprigs of mint, accompanied by the yoghurt dressing.

BAKED POTATO WITH TUNA AND MAYO

Real comfort food for family and friends, baked potatoes can be cooked in the air fryer in about half the time it would take to cook them in the oven. It requires hardly any pre-heating time either! If cooking 2, 3 or 4 baking potatoes, cooking timings remain the same.

Serves 1

Ingredients

1 medium baking potato
1 tsp olive oil
Salt and ground black pepper
Mixed salad, to serve

For the tuna filling

½ x 110g tin tuna in oil, drained
2 tbsp mayonnaise, ready-made or use recipe on page 101
½ tbsp snipped fresh chives
1 tsp lemon juice

1. Heat the air fryer to 200°C.

2. Scrub the potato, then blot dry between sheets of absorbent kitchen paper. Stand the potato on a chopping board and mark a cross in the top using a sharp vegetable knife. Using a pastry brush, brush all over with the olive oil and sprinkle with salt and pepper.

3. Transfer the potato to the air fryer basket and air-fry for 45–50 minutes, turning it over halfway through, until tender and golden.

4. Meanwhile, prepare the filling. In a medium mixing bowl, combine the tuna with the mayonnaise, chives, lemon juice and a seasoning of salt and pepper.

5. Remove the potato from the air fryer basket and, using a clean cloth, push it open from the base to form a waterlily shape.

6. Add the filling to the potato and serve with a mixed salad.

CURRIED CAULIFLOWER WITH CHEESE SAUCE

This tasty vegetable dish is simplicity itself to prepare and cook. Serve it as a side dish, or simply top it with a light cheese sauce to make it into a tasty main meal. You will need a large piece of foil here.

Serves 2

Ingredients

1 small cauliflower (approx. 350g)
Oil spray
1 tsp medium-hot curry powder
    (optional, but nice)
1 tbsp water
1 tsp sweet paprika
40g Cheddar cheese, grated
Salt and ground black pepper

For the cheese sauce

1 rounded tbsp cornflour
300ml semi-skimmed milk
1 tsp Dijon mustard
50g Gouda or Emmental cheese,
    grated

1. Heat the air fryer to 190°C.

2. Using either an apple corer or a sharp vegetable knife, carefully remove most of the core of the cauliflower, being careful to leave the cauliflower head intact.

3. Arrange the cauliflower, floret side up, in the centre of a large sheet of tin foil. Lightly spray with a little oil. Sprinkle with curry powder, if using, and paprika as well as a light seasoning of salt.

4. Add the water then enclose the cauliflower completely in the tin foil to make a parcel, with the join at the top. Place in the air-fryer basket and air-fry for 35 minutes.

5. Meanwhile, make the sauce. In a medium mixing bowl, combine the cornflour with about 2 tablespoons of the milk to make a smooth paste. Pour the remainder of the milk into a medium saucepan and heat until warm, over a medium heat on the hob. Pour the warm milk into the bowl with the blended cornflour and stir well. Season with salt and pepper. Return the sauce to the saucepan and bring to the boil, stirring continuously, until thickened. Remove from the heat and stir in the mustard and the grated cheese until melted. Keep warm.

6. Carefully partially unwrap the cauliflower to expose the head and sprinkle the Cheddar over the florets. Air-fry at 200°C for 2–3 minutes until the cheese is melted and golden.

7. Lift the cauliflower out of foil. Transfer to a serving dish and serve the cauliflower with the sauce poured over.

ROAST STUFFED PEPPERS

This is a great, easy lunch to enjoy with friends. I like to serve these accompanied by a mixed salad. Solo cooks might like to cook both peppers, as directed, chilling the second pepper. Reheat the following day, in the air fryer for approximately 3 minutes at 190°C.

Serves 2

Ingredients

1 red pepper

1 yellow pepper

110g packet flavoured couscous
   (I like lemon and coriander)

2 red or white spring onions,
   chopped

Oil spray

40g Parmesan cheese, grated
   (optional)

Mixed salad, to serve

1. Heat the air fryer to 200°C.

2. Cut the peppers in half vertically, leaving the stalks intact if preferred. Remove and discard the core and seeds.

3. To prepare the filling, make up the couscous according to the instructions on the packet. Cover and set aside for 10 minutes, then stir in the chopped spring onions.

4. Divide the filling evenly between the prepared pepper boats, then lightly spray each with a little oil. Place in the air fryer basket and air-fry for 5–6 minutes.

5. If you like, top with the grated Parmesan, and continue to air-fry for 2 minutes, until golden. Serve immediately with a mixed salad.

BROCCOLI, MUSHROOM AND RED ONION WITH SUNFLOWER SEEDS

A colourful vegetable dish that makes a great side and a useful addition to the buffet table. Adding a couple of sprays of water helps the broccoli to cook perfectly.

Serves 2

Ingredients
200g Tenderstem broccoli
175g button mushrooms, sliced
1 small red onion, sliced
1 tbsp olive oil
1 tsp chopped ginger, from a jar
1 tsp chopped garlic, from a jar
½ tsp chopped chillies, from a jar
1 tsp runny honey
Salt and ground black pepper
1 tbsp sunflower seeds, to serve

1. Heat the air fryer to 190°C.

2. Remove the woody stems from the broccoli and discard, then cut in half any thicker florets lengthways. Put the broccoli, mushrooms and red onion into a large mixing bowl.

3. In a small mug or bowl, combine the olive oil with the ginger, garlic, chillies and honey. Stir to combine, then pour over the vegetables and toss to coat evenly. Season with salt and pepper.

4. Turn the prepared vegetables into the air fryer basket and lightly spray with water. Air-fry for 4–5 minutes, shaking or turning the vegetables after 2 minutes. The broccoli needs to be slightly charred and cooked through. Discard any liquid left in the drawer of the air fryer or use it to make gravy or a sauce.

5. Transfer to a serving dish and sprinkle with the sunflower seeds.

CHEESY STUFFED MUSHROOMS

This recipe makes a great, healthy and filling lunch or supper dish that is quick and easy to prepare, and to cook in the air fryer. It's popular with almost everyone. Those with small air fryers might need to cook the mushrooms in batches. Serve with a tossed, mixed salad.

Serves 2

Ingredients

2 large flat mushrooms, such as
    Portobello
Oil spray
1 medium red pepper, deseeded
    and cut into small dice
1 medium courgette, chopped into
    small dice
3 spring onions (I like the red
    variety), sliced thinly
4 tbsp crème fraîche
1 tbsp chopped fresh parsley or
    1 tsp dried
40g Parmesan cheese, grated
25g Cheddar cheese, grated
Smoked sweet paprika, for dusting
Salt and ground black pepper
Mixed salad, to serve

1. Heat the air fryer to 190°C.

2. Remove the stems from the mushrooms and chop them finely. Transfer to a medium mixing bowl.

3. Stand the tops of the mushrooms on a chopping board, gill side down. Lightly spray each with a little oil. Turn the mushrooms over, exposing the gills.

4. Add to the mixing bowl the red pepper, courgette, spring onions, crème fraîche and the parsley. Season lightly with salt and pepper and mix well. Divide about half of the filling evenly between the mushrooms, then transfer the remainder to a salad bowl to serve alongside the cooked mushrooms.

5. Combine the cheeses and sprinkle over the stuffed mushrooms, dividing evenly. Dust each mushroom with a shake or 2 of paprika.

6. Stand the mushrooms, spaced apart, in the air fryer basket and air-fry for 7 minutes until golden.

7. Serve immediately, with the remaining red pepper and courgette mix and a mixed salad.

> **TIP:**
> Solo cooks might like to prepare and cook both mushrooms, chilling the second mushroom. Re-heat the next day for about 3 minutes at 190°C.

RATATOUILLE WITH MUSHROOMS AND HERBS

This colourful dish is particularly good during the autumn; it makes a filling side dish at any time of the year.

Serves 4

Ingredients

1 medium aubergine, roughly
    chopped
1 red pepper, deseeded and roughly
    chopped
1 yellow pepper, deseeded and
    roughly chopped
1 medium red onion, chopped
1 medium courgette, sliced
100g button mushrooms, sliced
1 large tomato, deseeded and
    roughly chopped
1 garlic clove, chopped
1 tbsp chopped fresh basil leaves or
    ½ tsp dried
2 tbsp olive oil
Salt and ground black pepper
Chopped fresh coriander or parsley,
    to serve

1. Heat the air fryer to 200°C.

2. In a large mixing bowl, toss all the vegetables together. Add the tomato, garlic, basil, olive oil and a light seasoning of salt and plenty of ground black pepper. Toss again to mix well.

3. Transfer to the air fryer basket and air-fry for 13–15 minutes, shaking the basket or stirring the vegetables after 6 and then 11 minutes.

4. Shake and serve, topped with plenty of chopped coriander or parsley.

MINI CHEESE AND CHIVE FILO TARTS

These individual cheese tarts are easy to make and quick to cook. A perfect meal to prepare when you have guests coming for brunch or lunch and haven't got much time. As these tarts freeze well for up to 3 months, I usually cook 4 even if I only need 2.

Serves 4

Accessories

4 ramekin dishes

Ingredients

20g melted butter

2 tbsp olive oil

4 sheets filo pastry approx.
34cm x 34cm, each cut into
4 equal squares

For the filling

3 large eggs

100ml single cream

½ tsp Dijon mustard

1 tbsp snipped fresh chives or
1 tsp dried mixed herbs

50g mature Cheddar cheese,
grated

2 cherry tomatoes, sliced

Salt and ground black pepper

1. Heat the air fryer to 170°C. Combine the melted butter with the olive oil and use a little to grease the ramekin dishes.

2. Place a filo square into each of the 4 ramekins, pushing it into the base and sides. Brush all over with a little butter and oil, then add another layer of pastry. Brush again with butter and oil. Continue until all the pastry sheets have been used up. Make sure you also oil the overhanging pastry.

3. Prepare the filling. In a mixing jug, combine the eggs with the cream, mustard and chives or mixed herbs. Beat well using a balloon whisk, then season with a little salt and plenty of pepper.

4. Divide the cheese between the raw pastry shells, then carefully pour the egg and cream mixture into each tart, on top of the cheese, dividing it evenly between the tarts. Add a few slices of tomato to each tart.

5. Cooking in batches, if necessary, transfer the ramekins to the air fryer basket and air-fry for 13–15 minutes, until the pastry is crisp and golden, and the custard is set in the middle.

FAMILY
LUNCHES

ROAST CHICKEN WITH LEMON AND ROSEMARY

A whole chicken, weighing 1.5kg, fits into most medium and large air fryer baskets without the top of the chicken touching the element. It cooks quicker than in a conventional oven, resulting in delicious crisp skin and moist flesh.

Serves 4

Accessories
Kitchen string
Roasting bag (optional)

Ingredients
1.5kg chicken, at room temperature
25g softened butter
1 tbsp Dijon mustard
1 tbsp olive oil
2 tsp juice from ½ lemon
  (keep the spent lemon)
1 tsp dried mixed herbs
2 sprigs of rosemary (optional)
Salt and ground black pepper

> ### TIP:
> To help keep your air fryer clean, cook the chicken in a biodegradable roasting bag.

1. Heat the air fryer to 180°C.

2. Blot the chicken dry with absorbent kitchen paper. Season the chicken all over with salt and pepper, rubbing it into the skin.

3. In a small mixing bowl, combine the butter, mustard, olive oil, lemon juice and mixed herbs. Smother this mixture all over the chicken breast and legs.

4. Put the squeezed lemon half and the sprigs of rosemary, if using, into the cavity of the chicken. Tie the legs together with the string. Place in the roasting bag, if using. Pour 75ml water in and seal with the metal tie provided.

5. Stand the chicken in the air fryer basket, breast side down. If not using a roasting bag, pour 75ml of water over the chicken, in the basket. Air-fry for 45 minutes, then carefully turn the chicken over so the breast is uppermost. Continue to air-fry for 10–20 minutes.

6. Remove the basket carefully and check that the chicken is cooked by piercing the thickest part of the thigh with a sharp vegetable knife. The juices must run clear, with no sign of blood. If necessary, return the chicken to the air fryer and air-fry for a further 2–3 minutes. The temperature of the chicken, when measured near to the thigh with a meat thermometer, must reach 82°C.

7. Remove the chicken and leave to rest, breast side up, covered with a tent of foil, for 20 minutes before carving.

8. Meanwhile, use any juices left in the base of the air fryer to make a delicious gravy.

ROAST LEG OF LAMB WITH ROSEMARY

Timings may vary according to your type of air fryer, but it is quick and easy to remove the drawer and check on the lamb. Don't forget, you are in control of how pink you like your lamb to be. Serve with the Roast new potatoes on page 122, freshly cooked vegetables, gravy and mint sauce.

Serves 3–4

Ingredients

1½ tsp chopped fresh rosemary leaves or use a mixture of fresh mint and rosemary leaves

1 tbsp olive oil

1kg extra-trimmed, boned and rolled leg of lamb, at room temperature

Salt and ground black pepper

To serve

Roast new potatoes (see page 122)
Cooked vegetables
Gravy
Mint sauce

1. Heat the air fryer to 180°C.

2. In a small bowl, combine the rosemary leaves with the olive oil and some salt and pepper.

3. Put the lamb on a chopping board and rub the seasoning paste all over the top of the lamb – this is easiest done with clean hands.

4. Put the lamb into the air fryer basket, herby side up. Air-fry for 10 minutes, then reduce the temperature to 170°C and continue to air-fry for 30–40 minutes until the lamb is cooked to your liking.

5. Remove from the air fryer and transfer to a chopping board. Leave to rest, covered with a tent of foil, for at least 20 minutes before carving.

6. Serve with roast new potatoes, vegetables, gravy and mint sauce.

BAKED GAMMON WITH CURRY SAUCE

This speedy-to-cook gammon is simply delicious served hot with the Hasselback potatoes on page 155. You can cook the potatoes in the air fryer while the ham is resting.

Serves 4–6

Accessories
2 large sheets of foil, 44cm long and 35cm wide

Ingredients
1kg boneless unsmoked gammon
1 celery stick, finely chopped
1 small onion, finely chopped
2 tsp mustard powder
2 tbsp orange juice
2 tsp runny honey
2 tsp demerara sugar
Ground black pepper
Hasselback potatoes (see page 155, to serve

For the curry sauce
4 tbsp crème fraîche
3 tbsp natural Greek yoghurt
2 tsp curry paste
1 tsp lemon juice
1 tbsp chopped fresh coriander
1 tsp runny honey

1. Take the gammon out of the fridge at least an hour before cooking.

2. Heat the air fryer to 170°C.

3. Lay the pieces of foil out on your worktop, to form a cross. Pile the celery and onion into the centre of the foil cross.

4. Stand the gammon on top of the vegetables. Season with ground black pepper. Wrap the gammon in the foil to make a sealed parcel, ensuring the overlapping join is at the top of the gammon joint. Transfer to the air fryer basket with the foil join uppermost. Air-fry for 40 minutes.

5. Meanwhile, in a small bowl, combine 1 teaspoon of the mustard powder with the orange juice and honey. Mix well.

6. After the 40 minutes, remove the basket from the air fryer, carefully open the parcel and pour over the honey glaze. Close the parcel and return to the air fryer for a further 20–25 minutes, until a meat thermometer inserted into the centre of the gammon reads 70°C.

7. Carefully transfer the cooked gammon to a chopping board and unwrap, just to expose the top of the joint. Set aside for a few minutes, to enable you to handle it. Using a sharp knife, remove the rind from the gammon and discard, then score the fat into a diamond pattern with the knife.

8. Combine the remaining teaspoon of mustard with the demerara sugar. Sprinkle this evenly over the scored fat.

9. Carefully return to the air fryer, leaving the fat exposed. Air-fry at 190°C for 7–8 minutes, checking after 5 minutes, until the fat is golden. Remove from the air fryer and set aside to rest, covered with a clean tent of foil, for 15–20 minutes, to tenderise, before carving.

10. Meanwhile, make the curry sauce. Put all the ingredients for the sauce into a medium mixing bowl and stir to blend. Taste and adjust the seasoning if necessary. Turn into a serving dish and serve with the gammon and Hasselback potatoes.

TIP:

Gammon joints take about 15 minutes per 450g in the air fryer.

SALMON AND COD FISH CAKES

This recipe makes an ideal lunch or supper. If preferred, the fish cakes can be prepared in the morning and chilled until ready to cook. To cook the raw fish, arrange both pieces of fish side by side in a microwaveable dish, adding a little salt and pepper and 1 tablespoon of water. Cover and microwave on full power for 3 minutes. Set aside for 4 minutes. Drain and use.

Serves 2

Ingredients

1 small carrot, sliced

100g white potatoes, peeled and
    cut into chunks

1 tbsp semi-skimmed milk

100g cooked skinless salmon fillet

75g cooked skinless cod fillet

1 tbsp chopped fresh parsley

Grated zest of ½ lemon

2 tbsp plain flour

1 small egg, beaten

2 tbsp panko breadcrumbs

Oil spray

Salt and ground black pepper

Cooked peas and carrots, to serve

1. Simmer the carrot and potatoes together in a covered pan of lightly salted boiling water for about 15 minutes, until completely tender. Drain and leave to steam dry for 2 minutes. Mash the potatoes and carrot well, then beat in the milk using a wooden spoon.

2. Lightly flake the cooked fish into the mashed potato and carrot, being careful not to break it up too much. Mix in the parsley and lemon zest. Season with salt and pepper. Using clean, damp hands, form the mixture into 2 fish cakes.

3. Put the flour, egg and breadcrumbs into 3 separate shallow cereal bowls. Dip each fish cake into the flour to coat, dust off any excess, then dip into the egg and finally coat in the breadcrumbs. Transfer to a plate and chill in the fridge for 20 minutes, or up to 5 hours. The fish cakes may also be wrapped and frozen at this stage, for up to 2 months.

4. Heat the air fryer to 190°C.

5. Lightly spray both sides of each fish cake with a little oil and lightly oil the air fryer basket. Arrange the fish cakes in the basket and air-fry for approximately 6 minutes, or until crisp and golden.

6. Using a fish slice, transfer the fish cakes to a serving dish. Serve with peas and carrots.

MARINATED CHICKEN DRUMSTICKS

These sticky drumsticks make a lovely mid-week family meal. Great for the kids to prepare and cook for their friends, good to take on a picnic, too. Serve with coleslaw and salad.

Makes 8 chicken drumsticks

Accessories (optional)
Basket liner

Ingredients
8 chicken drumsticks
2 tsp olive oil
4 tbsp tomato ketchup
1 tbsp runny honey
1 tsp soy sauce
2 tsp smoked sweet paprika
1 tsp chopped chillies, from a jar
1 tsp chopped ginger, from a jar
1 tsp chopped garlic, from a jar
Oil spray
Salt and ground black pepper

To serve
Coleslaw
Mixed salad

1. Pat the chicken drumsticks dry between sheets of absorbent kitchen paper.

2. In a large mixing bowl, combine the olive oil, tomato ketchup, honey, soy sauce, paprika, chillies, ginger and garlic. Add a light seasoning of salt and plenty of ground black pepper. Stir well.

3. Add the drumsticks to the bowl and using a wooden spoon, or your hands, mix well to ensure the drumsticks are well coated with the sauce. Set aside for 15 minutes, to allow the flavours to mingle. Alternatively, cover the bowl and chill for several hours or overnight.

4. Heat the air fryer to 200°C.

5. Place a liner in the base of the basket or lightly spray the basket with oil. Add the drumsticks to the basket. Air-fry for 10–12 minutes, then shake the basket or turn each drumstick over. Return to the air fryer at 160°C and cook for 10 minutes, until slightly blackened and cooked through. Remove using kitchen tongs.

6. Serve with coleslaw and a mixed salad.

PORK AND APPLE BURGERS

The air fryer cooks these tasty pork burgers to perfection. Serve in brioche buns, with a tomato, red onion and mixed herb salad.

Serves 2

Ingredients

250g pork mince

25g fresh brown breadcrumbs

½ tsp dried mixed herbs

½ small dessert apple, grated

2 spring onions, chopped

1 tsp sweet paprika

2 tsp Dijon mustard

½ egg, lightly beaten

Oil spray

Salt and ground black pepper

2 Brioche buns

Tomato, red onion and lettuce,
  to serve

1. Heat the air fryer to 200°C.

2. In a large mixing bowl, combine the pork mince with the breadcrumbs, mixed herbs, apple, spring onions, sweet paprika and mustard. Add a seasoning of salt and pepper.

3. Mix well to combine, then add the egg to bind the mixture together. Form into 2 flattish burgers.

4. Spray the basket with a little oil and add the burgers to the basket. Cook for approximately 8 minutes, flipping after 4 minutes, until cooked to your liking. Serve with salad or fries.

MANGO CHUTNEY-GLAZED CHICKEN THIGHS WITH SIMPLE SLAW

These sticky chicken thighs are absolutely delicious when served with the simple slaw. A great dish for lunch or supper.

Serves 2

Ingredients

2 tsp Dijon mustard

1 tsp medium curry powder

1 tsp fennel seeds

1 tsp dried coriander or dried mixed herbs

1 tbsp mango chutney

1 tbsp olive oil

2 large chicken thigh fillets

Oil Spray

Salt and ground black pepper

Fresh mango, chopped (optional)

For the simple slaw

About ¼ medium white or red cabbage, shredded

50g carrots, grated

1 celery stick, chopped

2 red or white spring onions, chopped

2 tbsp natural Greek yoghurt

2 tsp curry paste

1 tbsp mayonnaise

2 tsp lemon juice

Handful of dried cranberries

50g pecan nuts, chopped

1. To make the glaze, combine the mustard with the curry powder, fennel seeds, coriander or mixed herbs, mango chutney and olive oil in a mixing bowl. Add a seasoning of salt and pepper. Stir well.

2. Open out the thigh fillets and add to the bowl. Using clean hands, massage the glaze into the chicken gently. Cover the bowl and set aside for 15 minutes for the flavours to mingle, or cover and chill overnight.

3. Heat the air fryer to 180°C.

4. Lightly oil the air fryer basket. Place the prepared chicken into the air fryer basket and air-fry for about 15–20 minutes, until the chicken is cooked through. Allow to rest for a few minutes while you make the slaw.

5. Put all the ingredients for the slaw, except the nuts, into a large mixing bowl. Toss well to coat everything with the yoghurt and mayonnaise mixture. Season with salt and pepper to taste. Transfer to a serving dish and serve topped with the pecan nuts, alongside the chicken and freshly chopped mango.

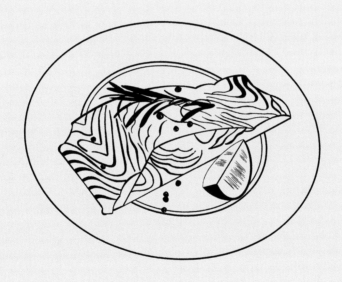

SIMPLE
SUPPERS

CHICKEN AND PORTOBELLO MUSHROOM FAJITAS

Fajitas are my go-to meal at the local pub, so I make this version at home, which is so easy to cook in the air fryer.

Serves 2

Ingredients

1 large field mushroom, thickly
    sliced
Oil spray
250g chicken breast fillet, sliced
½ red pepper, deseeded and thinly
    sliced
½ yellow pepper, deseeded and
    thinly sliced
1 small red onion, sliced
1 tbsp olive oil
2 tbsp fajita seasoning, from a jar
Salt

To serve

4 flour tortillas
Soured cream
Shredded lettuce
Chopped tomatoes
1 ripe avocado, stoned and mashed
    with a little lime juice

1. Heat the air fryer to 190°C.

2. Lay the sliced mushroom on a chopping board and spray lightly with a little oil.

3. In a medium mixing bowl, put the chicken, red and yellow peppers, onion and mushroom slices. Add the olive oil and the fajita seasoning, plus a light seasoning of salt. Toss to coat, using 2 spoons.

4. Lightly oil the air fryer basket. Transfer the contents of the bowl to the basket and spread out as much as possible. Air-fry for 5 minutes, then shake the basket or stir the ingredients. Continue to air-fry for 2–3 minutes, until the chicken and vegetables are cooked.

5. Shake, then serve with the tortillas, soured cream, lettuce, tomatoes and mashed avocado.

SAUSAGES WITH ROAST CARROTS AND NEW POTATOES

This tasty supper dish is delicious, very popular with the kids, and so quick and easy to make.

Serves 2

Ingredients
2 carrots, sliced
150g small new potatoes, halved
1 tbsp sunflower oil
1 tsp dried parsley
4 chipolata sausages
Salt and ground black pepper

1. Heat the air fryer to 190°C.

2. Put all the ingredients, except the sausages, into a large mixing bowl. Season with salt and pepper. Toss to coat in the oil.

3. Transfer the contents of the bowl to the air fryer basket and air-fry for 10 minutes. Shake the basket, then lay the sausages on top of the vegetables, spaced out a little.

4. Continue to air-fry at 190°C for 5–7 minutes, until the sausages and vegetables are nicely golden and cooked through. Shake and serve.

FROZEN FISH FINGERS AND CHIPS WITH FENNEL SLAW

A delicious speedy supper that is great for both the children and grandchildren. The coleslaw is pretty to look at and is full of healthy goodness. Soaking the onion in vinegar for a few minutes makes it milder and softer.

Serves 2

Ingredients
Oil spray
450g frozen crinkle cut chips
6 frozen fish fingers

For the fennel slaw
½ small red onion, finely sliced
2 tsp red wine vinegar
½ fennel bulb, finely sliced
1 small carrot, grated
¼ small red or white cabbage, shredded
1 small red-skinned eating apple, cored and chopped
Grated zest and juice of ½ orange
1 tbsp crème fraîche
2 tbsp natural Greek yoghurt
1 tbsp Dijon mustard
Salt and ground black pepper
Pecan nuts, chopped, to serve

1. Heat the air fryer to 200°C.

2. To prevent sticking, lightly spray the basket with a little oil. Put the frozen chips straight into the air fryer basket. Air-fry for 9 minutes, then shake gently. Carefully add the frozen fish fingers, spaced apart, and coat with 4 sprays of oil. Continue to air-fry for 7–10 minutes, until the chips are crisp and golden and the fish fingers are cooked through, also crisp and golden.

3. While the chips and fish fingers are cooking, make the slaw. Start by putting the onion into a small bowl with the vinegar and allow it to soften for about 5 minutes while you get on with preparing the rest of the slaw. Put the fennel, carrot and cabbage into a large mixing bowl and add the apple, orange zest and juice, crème fraîche, yoghurt and mustard. Toss together to mix well. Drain the onion, then rinse in cold water, drain again and add to the bowl. Season with salt and pepper to taste, then toss again. Turn into a serving bowl.

4. Top the slaw with the pecan nuts and serve alongside the fish fingers and chips.

BEEF MEATBALLS WITH FETA AND HERBS

This delicious family meal has become a real favourite in our household. Use a lightly oiled liner if you have one, to prevent the meatballs sticking to the base of the basket. Serve with freshly cooked pasta and a tomato sauce.

Serves 4
Makes 12 meatballs

Accessories
Basket liner and metal rack
    (optional, see method)

Ingredients
350g lean beef mince, at room
    temperature
200g lean pork sausage meat,
    at room temperature
1 small red onion, grated or finely
    chopped
1 garlic clove, crushed
1 tbsp chopped fresh parsley
1 tbsp chopped fresh coriander
2 tsp sweet paprika
25g fresh brown breadcrumbs
50g feta cheese, chopped
1 medium egg, lightly beaten
Salt and ground black pepper
Pasta, freshly cooked
Ready-made tomato sauce

1. Heat the air fryer to 180°C.

2. In a large mixing bowl, combine all the ingredients, except the egg and seasoning. Season with a little salt and plenty of pepper and add the beaten egg. Mix well.

3. Using clean, damp hands, roll the mixture into 12 meatballs, each about the size of a golf ball. Arrange the meatballs in a single layer, on a liner in the air fryer basket. For those with smaller air fryers, use a metal rack. Do not allow the meatballs to touch. If necessary, cook the meatballs in 2 batches. Air-fry each batch, for 11–14 minutes, until cooked through and browned.

4. Serve immediately.

SALMON WITH SOY SAUCE AND LEMON

A delicious meal for 2 that is great served with a colourful array of vegetables, such as carrots, broccoli and peas.

Serves 2

Ingredients

1 tbsp soy sauce
2 tsp fresh lemon juice
½ tsp dried mixed herbs
2 x 125g salmon fillets, skin on
2 spring onions, chopped
Oil spray
Ground black pepper
Freshly cooked vegetables, to serve

1. In a small mixing bowl, combine the soy sauce, lemon juice and mixed herbs. Add a seasoning of freshly ground black pepper and stir to mix.

2. Arrange the salmon fillets side by side, skin side down, in a suitable shallow dish. Pour the marinade over the salmon and set aside for 10 minutes.

3. Heat the air fryer to 190°C.

4. Lift the salmon from the marinade and arrange in a single layer in the air fryer basket, skin side down. Sprinkle over the chopped spring onions.

5. Lightly spray each salmon fillet with a little oil. Air-fry for 7 minutes, or until the salmon is cooked to your liking. Serve with freshly cooked vegetables.

CHICKEN BREAST TRAY BAKE

A healthy alternative to the Sunday roast. Particularly light and refreshing during summer months.

Serves 2

Accessories (optional)
Liner

Ingredients
2 small chicken breast fillets
  (about 300g), diced
Juice of ½ lemon
1 medium tomato, roughly chopped
1 courgette, sliced
1 red pepper, deseeded and sliced
1 small red onion, sliced
1 garlic clove, chopped
1 tsp dried mixed herbs
2 tsp olive oil
1 tsp sweet paprika
1 tsp medium curry powder
Salt

1. Heat the air fryer to 190°C.

2. Blot the chicken dry between sheets of absorbent kitchen paper. Then put the chicken into a large mixing bowl and squeeze the lemon juice over. Toss to coat.

3. Put the tomato and vegetables into a second large mixing bowl and add the garlic, herbs, olive oil, paprika, curry powder and a little salt. Toss to coat.

4. Add the vegetables and chicken, muddled together, to the air fryer basket. Air-fry for 10–12 minutes, removing and shaking basket or gently stirring the ingredients, every 4 minutes. The chicken must be cooked through and both chicken and vegetables need to be slightly charred and aromatic. Serve.

BUTTERED PLAICE WITH HOMEMADE MAYONNAISE

Serve with green beans and the Sauté potatoes on page 148, which should be cooked before you cook the fish. When the fish is cooked, you can reheat the potatoes in the air fryer at 200°C for 2–3 minutes. It is well worth making this delicious mayonnaise, which stores well in the fridge for up to 5 days. Should you wish to cook 2 plaice fillets at same time, the cooking time remains as given.

Serves 1

Accessories
Ramekin
Liner, (optional)

Ingredients
2 tsp butter
2 tsp lemon juice
Oil spray
1 medium plaice fillet
2 tsp chopped fresh parsley
Salt and ground black pepper

For the mayonnaise
1 large egg
1–2 tsp Dijon mustard
2 tsp lemon juice, or to taste
240ml sunflower oil

To serve
Cooked green beans
Sauté potatoes (see page 148)

1. Heat the air fryer to 160°C.

2. First prepare the mayonnaise. In a tall jam jar or narrow jug, which will fit a stick blender head, combine the egg, mustard and lemon juice. Pour the oil on top and set aside for about 10 seconds for the oil to settle. Put the stick blender into the jar, making sure it touches the base of the jar. Blend at high speed, but don't move the machine. As the mayonnaise forms, slowly tilt the head of the stick blender, until all the oil is incorporated into the egg. Season the mayonnaise with salt and pepper, plus more lemon juice, to taste. Transfer to a covered container and store in the fridge for up to 5 days.

3. To cook the fish, melt the butter in a small ramekin in the air fryer, for 1–2 minutes. Remove from the air fryer and add the lemon juice. Season with a little salt and pepper. Mix well.

4. Heat the air fryer to 180°C.

5. Spray the air fryer basket with a little oil or use a lightly oiled liner. Carefully lay the plaice fillet in the basket, then brush all over with the melted butter and sprinkle with a little parsley. Air-fry for about 4 minutes, until cooked through and golden.

6. Using a fish slice, transfer the cooked fish to a serving plate. Serve immediately, accompanied by the mayonnaise and green beans and sauté potatoes.

EASY CURRIED SALMON

This recipe can be easily halved to serve 2 people. The cooking time remains as given. The fish is marinated in a spicy sauce before being cooked quickly in the air fryer. A delicious dish to serve to guests with freshly prepared couscous and steamed broccoli or kale.

Serves 4

Ingredients

3 tbsp natural Greek yoghurt

1 tbsp curry paste of your choice

1 tbsp coriander, freshly chopped
    or 2 tsp dried

1 tsp lemon juice

4 salmon fillets

1 lemon, sliced

Oil spray

Salt

Couscous and steamed broccoli or
    kale, to serve

1. In a medium mixing bowl, combine the yoghurt with the curry paste, coriander and lemon juice. Stir in a light seasoning of salt.

2. Arrange the salmon in a suitable shallow dish that will hold the fish in a single layer. Pour the marinade over to coat the fish. Set aside for 15 minutes to allow the flavours to mingle.

3. Heat the air fryer to 200°C.

4. Top each salmon fillet with a thin slice of lemon and lightly spray each fillet with a little oil. Lightly oil the air fryer basket. Transfer the salmon to the air fryer basket and air-fry for 6–7 minutes, or until the salmon is cooked to your liking.

5. Serve immediately, with couscous and steamed vegetables.

PORK SAUSAGES AND CHIPS

Starting out with my air fryer, I was amazed at the speed at which it cooked good-quality chilled pork sausages and frozen chips, together, and to perfection every time. If cooking for 2 people, simply double the ingredients. Cooking time remains the same as given.

Serves 1

Ingredients

250g frozen crinkle cut oven chips
2 pork chipolata sausages (at least
    60% pork), from the fridge
Carrot sticks or baked beans,
    to serve

1. Heat the air fryer to 190°C.

2. Tip the chips straight from the freezer into the air fryer basket. Place the sausages, evenly spaced out, on top of the chips. Air-fry for 4 minutes.

3. Remove the basket, then shake, or stir and turn the contents and return to the air fryer.

4. Air-fry at 200°C for about 8 minutes, until the chips are crisp and golden, and the sausages are cooked.

5. Serve immediately with carrot sticks or baked beans.

CHICKEN BREASTS WITH ROSEMARY AND BACON

This healthy, yet delicious meal can be cooked in the air fryer in about 20 minutes. Serve with mashed potato and a mixed side salad.

Serves 2

Accessories
4 wooden cocktail sticks

Ingredients
2 x 120g skinless chicken breast
  fillets
1 tsp olive oil
1 tbsp Cajun seasoning
2 rashers back bacon
Oil spray
Sprigs of rosemary
Mashed potato
Mixed salad, to serve

1. Heat the air fryer to 180°C.

2. Blot the chicken breasts dry between sheets of absorbent kitchen paper. Brush the chicken all over with the olive oil, then sprinkle with the Cajun seasoning. Set aside for 10 minutes or so, to allow the flavours to penetrate. Wrap each chicken breast in a rasher of bacon. Secure with wooden cocktail sticks.

3. Spray the base of the air fryer basket with a little oil, then lay the sprigs of rosemary, spaced apart, in the basket. Spray the rosemary with a light mist of water and top each sprig with a wrapped chicken breast.

4. Air-fry for 15–18 minutes, or until the centre of chicken reaches 82°C when measured with a meat thermometer or the juice runs clear, with no sign of blood, when pierced with a sharp knife.

5. Leave to rest for 5 minutes, then slice the chicken and serve with mashed potato and a mixed salad.

TIP:
Solo cooks might like to cook the 2 bacon-wrapped chicken breasts, chilling the cooked, extra portion to use the next day. Re-heat in the air fryer at 190°C for approximately 5 minutes, or until hot in centre.

ONE POT CHICKEN AND RICE

A great, Cajun-inspired recipe that is full of flavour and really easy to cook in the air fryer.

Serves 4

Accessories

Baking tin, approx. 18cm square x
    8cm deep, or a large soufflé dish

Ingredients

1 tbsp olive oil

2 chicken breast fillets, diced

Oil spray

1 shallot, diced

1 red pepper, deseeded and diced

1 tbsp Cajun seasoning

2 garlic cloves, crushed, or 1 tsp
    chopped garlic, from a jar

200g basmati rice, washed and
    drained

400g tin chopped tomatoes

350ml hot chicken or vegetable
    stock

Chopped fresh coriander, to
    garnish

Chopped fresh chilli, to garnish

Mixed salad, to serve

1. Heat the air fryer to 190°C.

2. Heat the oil in the base of the baking tin or soufflé dish, in the air fryer, for 2 minutes.

3. Spray the chicken breasts with a little oil and add the chicken and shallot to the air fryer basket. Stir together, then air-fry for 5 minutes.

4. Add the red pepper, Cajun seasoning and the garlic and air-fry for 2 minutes.

5. Stir in the rice, tomatoes and stock.
Cover the dish tightly with foil and air-fry at 180°C for 30 minutes.

6. Remove the dish from the air fryer and stand, covered, for 5–8 minutes. Stir and serve, sprinkled with the coriander, and accompanied by a salad.

TURKEY AND BACON BURGERS

This is a great meal for older kids to prepare and cook themselves. I like to make the burgers slightly flatter than you might do normally, to help them cook evenly and quickly.

Serves 2

Accessories (optional)
Liner

Ingredients
200g turkey mince
1 tbsp porridge oats
1 tbsp chopped fresh coriander
1 rasher streaky bacon, chopped
1 tsp wholegrain mustard
2 red or white spring onions, chopped
1 tsp sweet paprika
Oil spray
Salt and ground black pepper
2 Brioche buns, to serve
Salad or coleslaw, to serve

1. Heat the air fryer to 190°C.

2. In a large mixing bowl, combine the turkey mince with the porridge oats, coriander, bacon, mustard and spring onions. Mix well to combine, adding a seasoning of salt and pepper and the paprika.

3. Shape into 2 flattish burgers using damp, clean hands. Put an oiled liner into the air fryer basket, or lightly oil the basket. Add the burgers, not touching, and air-fry for about 10 minutes, until browned and cooked through.

4. Serve immediately in a brioche bun, with a salad or coleslaw.

TIP:
Solo cooks might like to cook both burgers, chilling the second burger for the next day. Re-heat at 190°C for approximately 5 minutes, or until piping hot in centre.

SPEEDY PORK AND TURKEY MEATBALLS

The air fryer makes cooking meatballs so easy, with no fear of burning the outsides before the centre is cooked. Serve with rice, broccoli and the easy tomato and butternut squash sauce opposite.

Serves 4
Makes 12 meatballs

Accessories (optional)
Liner

Ingredients
250g pork mince
250g turkey breast or leg mince
25g fresh brown breadcrumbs
1 tbsp chopped fresh parsley
1 small dessert apple, cored and
    grated
1 small red onion, finely chopped
2 tsp sweet paprika
2 tsp wholegrain or Dijon mustard
1 large egg, beaten
Oil spray
Salt and ground black pepper
Mixed salad and tomato sauce (see
    opposite), to serve

1. Heat the air fryer to 200°C.

2. In a large mixing bowl, combine all the ingredients except for the egg. Season with salt and pepper. Mix well with a wooden spoon, just to combine. Add the beaten egg and, using damp, clean hands, mix well. Form the mixture into 12 meatballs, each about the size of a golf ball.

3. Line the air fryer with a lightly oiled liner or spray the basket base with a little oil. Add the meatballs in a single layer – or you may prefer to cook in 2 batches. Air-fry for 10–15 minutes, until browned and cooked through.

4. Serve immediately, with the mixed salad and tomato sauce.

EASY TOMATO AND BUTTERNUT SQUASH SAUCE

Serves 4

Ingredients

2 tbsp olive oil

2 red onions, chopped

1 garlic clove, chopped,
   or 1 tsp chopped garlic,
   from a jar

1 tbsp tomato purée

½ butternut squash, deseeded,
   peeled and cut into cubes

500g carton tomato passata

100ml vegetable stock

1 tsp runny honey

2 tbsp chopped fresh basil or
   1 tsp dried

Salt and ground black pepper

1. Heat the oil in a large saucepan on the hob. Stir in the onions and cook for about 7 minutes over a medium heat, stirring frequently, until they soften and turn golden. Stir in the garlic and the butternut squash. Cook, stirring, for 1 minute.

2. Add the passata, tomato purée, stock, honey, basil and salt and pepper. Simmer, covered with a lid and stirring now and again, for 20–25 minutes until the butternut squash is tender.

3. Serve immediately with meatballs.

DINING IN

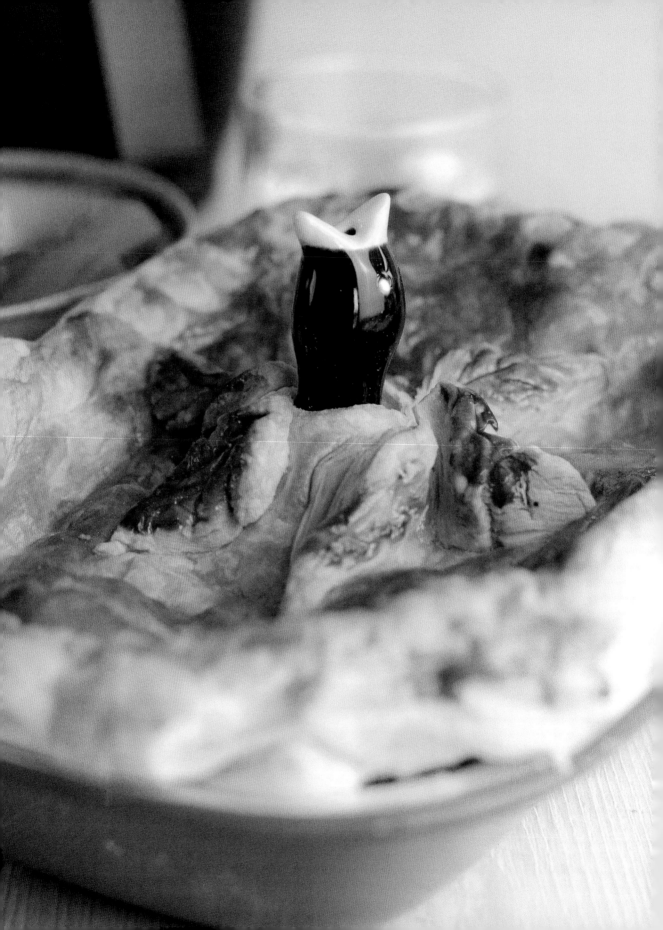

PUFF PASTRY MEAT PIE

This delicious meat pie, with a crisp pastry topping, uses the leftovers from your roast – whether a chicken or a joint of pork, lamb or beef.

Serves 2

Accessories
Pyrex or metal pie dish (approx.
    19cm x 13cm wide x 4cm deep)
Foil sling (see page 18)

Ingredients
300g leftover meat from a roast
    (pork, lamb, beef or chicken),
    roughly chopped
150ml leftover gravy, thick enough
    to coat the meat and vegetables
75g leftover cooked carrots
320g sheet rolled puff pastry
1 small egg, beaten
Steamed cabbage and carrots,
    to serve

1. Heat the air fryer to 180°C.

2. In a mixing bowl, combine the leftover meat with the gravy and cooked carrots. Stir gently, then turn into a pie dish.

3. Cut the pastry to fit the pie dish, then use the excess to cut a thin strip, about 2cm wide. Brush the rim of the pie dish with cold water, then add the pastry strip. Moisten the pastry strip with cold water, then top with the pastry lid. Seal, then crimp the edges. Slash 2 small holes in the top of the pie, to allow steam to escape. Brush all over with the beaten egg.

4. Put the pie into the air fryer basket and air-fry for 20–25 minutes, until the pastry is well risen and golden and the filling in the centre is hot.

5. Serve with steamed cabbage and carrots.

SCALLOPS WRAPPED IN BACON

An ideal dish to serve as a canapé with pre-dinner drinks, or as a main meal with jacket potatoes and salad. If you buy large scallops from a fishmonger, you will only need 10. Cut them in half, before wrapping in bacon.

Serves 4
Makes 20 canapés

Accessories
Ramekin
20 wooden cocktail sticks

Ingredients
25g butter
20 scallops or 180g packet of
    frozen scallops, defrosted
10 slices streaky bacon, cut in half
About 2 tbsp olive oil mixed with
    1 tsp chopped fresh parsley or
    ½ tsp dried
Samphire, to serve

1. Heat the air fryer to 160°C and melt the butter in a ramekin for 2 minutes.

2. Blot the scallops and the bacon dry between sheets of absorbent kitchen paper, then lay the half slices of bacon out on a chopping board and stretch them out using the back of a knife.

3. Spread half of the bacon in the air fryer basket, in a single layer, and air-fry at 190°C for 3 minutes. Remove from the air fryer, using tongs, and place on the chopping board in a single layer. Allow to cool. Repeat with the remaining bacon.

4. Wrap each scallop in a half rasher of the par-cooked bacon. Secure with a cocktail stick. Repeat until all the bacon and scallops have been prepared. Brush the tops of each rolled scallop with a little of the herby olive oil.

5. Cook the scallops in 2 batches. Put half into the basket, making sure they are not touching, and air-fry at 200°C for approximately 6 minutes. The scallops are ready when they are no longer opaque and the bacon is crisp and smelling amazing! Repeat with the second batch.

6. Serve immediately, sprinkled with the samphire.

CRISPY GARLIC PRAWNS

Use a lightly oiled perforated liner to help keep your air fryer basket clean and stop breadcrumbs falling into the base of the air fryer. These popular crispy prawns make a delicious hot starter or canapé to serve with drinks. Take care not to overcook the prawns as they will become tough.

Serves 2

Accessories (optional)
Liner

Ingredients
150g peeled and de-veined large
   raw prawns (defrosted if frozen)
2 tbsp plain flour
1 large egg, beaten
2 tbsp panko breadcrumbs
Oil spray
Salt and ground black pepper

1. Heat the air fryer to 200°C.

2. If the prawns have been defrosted, blot them dry between sheets of absorbent kitchen paper.

3. Put the flour, egg and breadcrumbs into 3 separate shallow cereal bowls. Season the flour with a little salt and pepper. Working a few at a time, coat each prawn with the flour, then dip into the egg, and finally toss in the breadcrumbs until completely coated. Shake off any surplus breadcrumbs. Place the prawns, spaced apart, on a plate and lightly spray on both sides with a little oil.

4. Place an oiled liner into the air fryer basket, then add the prepared prawns. Don't overcrowd the basket; you may need to cook the prawns in 2 batches.

5. Air-fry for 3 minutes, then shake gently or turn the prawns over. Air-fry for 2–4 minutes more, until crisp and golden. Continue until all the prawns have been cooked. Best served hot or warm.

RUMP STEAK WITH ASPARAGUS

Don't be scared to cook steak in the air fryer; it works well, with less washing up afterwards. Make use of the delicious meat juices that drip into the base of the air fryer basket and pour them over the cooked steaks on serving. Enjoy with steamed new potatoes and coleslaw.

Serves 2

Ingredients

2 rump steaks, each about 250g,
    at room temperature for at least
    1 hour
2 tsp Dijon mustard
Oil spray
350g fresh asparagus, woody ends
    snapped off
Salt and ground black pepper

To serve

Steamed new potatoes
Coleslaw (page 88 and 95)

1. Heat the air fryer to 200°C.

2. Put the steaks on a chopping board and pound, using either a steak hammer or the end of a rolling pin, to tenderise. Season with salt and pepper and spread each of the steaks with a teaspoon of mustard. Lightly spray each steak, on both sides, with a little oil.

3. Lightly oil the air fryer basket. Place the steaks in the air fryer basket, not quite touching. For medium, air-fry for 7–8 minutes, flipping each steak over after 4 minutes. Air fry for about 8 minutes each side, if you prefer your steak well done. Remove from the air fryer and transfer to a warm plate. Leave to rest for at least 10 minutes.

4. Put the asparagus into the air fryer basket and spray with about 5 sprays of oil. Season with a little salt and pepper. Air-fry for 5 minutes at 200°C, until lightly charred.

5. Remove from the basket and serve immediately with the steak, new potatoes and coleslaw.

ROAST RACK OF LAMB WITH ROAST NEW POTATOES

This delicious joint cooks to perfection in the air fryer in minutes; the timings here are for lamb cooked to medium. You can ask the butcher to French trim the lamb for you. Serve with a salad of young spinach and torn little gem leaves, chopped mint leaves, chopped tomatoes and diced cucumber, tossed together in a little vinaigrette dressing.

Serves 4

Ingredients

850g lean rack of lamb,
   French trimmed and at room
   temperature
2 tbsp olive oil
1½ tsp dried mixed herbs
300g new potatoes, cut in half
2 tsp sweet paprika
Salt and ground black pepper

To serve

Mint sauce
Gravy (optional)
Mixed salad (see intro)

1. Heat the air fryer to 190°C.

2. Pat the lamb dry between sheets of absorbent kitchen paper. Score the fat into a diamond pattern using a sharp knife, then rub 2 teaspoons of the olive oil into the fat and season the lamb all over with a little salt and pepper. Rub 1 teaspoon of the dried herbs into the fat.

3. Put the potatoes into a mixing bowl and add the remaining olive oil, a seasoning of salt and pepper and the paprika. Toss together and turn into the air fryer basket.

4. Place the lamb, fat side up, on top of the potatoes. Air-fry for 20–30 minutes, or until the lamb is cooked to your liking, and the potatoes are crisp and golden.

5. Transfer the rack of lamb to a warm plate and leave to rest, covered with a tent of foil, for 15 minutes before serving. Leave the potatoes in the air fryer, with the machine switched off.

6. Carve the rested lamb into chops and serve with the crisp potatoes, some mint sauce, gravy and the mixed salad.

RUMP STEAKS WITH TOMATOES AND CORN ON THE COB

Steak and tomatoes make a good combination and cook well together. The steak will be cooked to medium. Cook the sweetcorn first, then steam or boil some new potatoes on the hob while you are cooking the steak.

Serves 2

Ingredients

2 small sweetcorn cobs, at room
    temperature
Oil spray
2 x 180g rump steaks, at room
    temperature
2 tsp mustard powder (optional)
2 small tomatoes, halved
    horizontally
Salt and ground black pepper
Boiled new potatoes, to serve

1. Heat the air fryer to 190°C.

2. Spray the sweetcorn cobs all over with about 5 sprays of the oil. Sprinkle with a little salt and pepper, then put into the air fryer basket. Air-fry for 8–10 minutes, shaking the basket gently after 5 minutes. Shake once more before transferring to a warm serving dish, then set aside, covered with a tent of foil to keep warm.

3. Meanwhile, prepare the steaks. Arrange the steaks on a chopping board and bash all over with either a steak hammer or the end of a wooden rolling pin, to tenderise. Season on both sides with a little salt and pepper, then rub the tops of each steak with the mustard, if using, dividing it equally between them. Spray both sides of the steaks with a little oil.

4. Put the steaks and tomatoes into the air fryer basket. Spray the tomatoes with a little oil and season with salt and pepper. Air-fry for 6–7 minutes, turning the steaks over after 3 minutes. Remove from the air fryer and allow to rest for 5 minutes, to allow the steaks to tenderise.

5. Serve the steaks, with any pan juices poured over, accompanied by the tomatoes, with the sweetcorn and some boiled new potatoes.

PORK CHOPS WITH CHIVES, COURGETTE AND RED PEPPER

Solo cooks might like to cook the chops with the vegetables, then set aside the second portion, covered, in the fridge ready to re-heat later in the air fryer. When ready to re-heat, place in a small Pyrex or similar dish, covered with foil, and return to the air fryer for approximately 5 minutes at 190°C. Serve the chops with peas and some apple sauce.

Serves 2

Ingredients

1 medium courgette, sliced

1 small red pepper, deseeded and
   sliced

1 tbsp olive oil

1 tsp lemon juice

1 tsp runny honey

1 tsp Dijon or wholegrain mustard

A few snipped chives

2 boneless, lean pork loin chops
   (each about 130g)

Oil Spray

Salt and ground black pepper

Cooked peas and apple sauce,
   to serve

1. In a medium mixing bowl, combine the courgette and red pepper with the olive oil, lemon juice, honey, mustard, chives and a seasoning of salt and pepper and stir gently. Lay the chops on top and stir again, just so that some of the ingredients coat the pork as well. Cover and set aside for 10 minutes, to allow the flavours to mingle.

2. Heat the air fryer to 200°C.

3. Using tongs, transfer the chops to a plate. Lightly oil the air fryer basket. Toss the vegetables into the air fryer basket. Lay the chops, evenly spaced apart, on top. Air-fry for 5 minutes, then turn over the chops and continue to air-fry for a further 4–6 minutes, or until the pork is golden and cooked through and the vegetables are lightly charred. Remove the basket from the air fryer and leave to stand for 5 minutes.

4. Serve with peas and apple sauce.

SPATCHCOCK CHICKEN

Ready-prepared spatchcock chicken is available in large supermarkets. Alternatively, ask your butcher to spatchcock the bird for you. Serve with carrots, spinach and Roast new potatoes on page 122 which can be cooked in the air-fryer, while the chicken rests.

Serves 4

Ingredients

1 spatchcocked chicken (about
   1.5kg) at room temperature
   for 40 minutes
1 tbsp olive oil
15g softened butter
1 tbsp Creole seasoning or
   chicken seasoning of your choice
1 tsp smoked sweet paprika
1 tsp dried mixed herbs
Salt and ground black pepper

To serve

Cooked carrots and spinach
Roast new potatoes (see page 122)

1. Heat the air fryer to 180°C.

2. Pat the chicken dry between sheets of absorbent kitchen paper.

3. Place the chicken, skin side up, on a chopping board. Using a pastry brush, coat the chicken all over with the oil. Spread over the butter. Using your clean hands, rub the spices and herbs into the chicken skin. Season with salt and pepper.

4. Carefully transfer the chicken to the air-fryer basket, skin side down. Air-fry for 30–40 minutes, flipping the chicken over after 15 minutes, or until the juices run clear when the thickest part of the chicken is pierced with a sharp knife (as for other chicken recipes).

5. Remove the chicken from the basket and rest, covered with a tent of foil, for 15 minutes, before carving.

6. Serve with freshly cooked carrots and spinach and some roast new potatoes.

STUFFED SEA BASS WITH LEMON

As the fish is baked in foil parcels, all the nutrients, as well as the flavour, are served up on the plate. Only use foil if your manufacturer endorses its use, otherwise, cook each of the sea bass in a roasting bag.

Serves 2

Ingredients

Oil spray

2 sea bass, cleaned and gutted, head and tail removed

¼ fennel bulb, finely sliced

1 medium tomato, deseeded and chopped

2 green pitted olives, chopped

1 tbsp chopped fresh parsley

1 garlic clove, crushed

1 lemon, sliced, plus wedges to serve

2 tbsp dry cider or water

Salt and ground black pepper

Salad, to serve (see method)

1. Heat the air fryer to 190°C.

2. Arrange each of the prepared sea bass on 2 large, individual squares of oiled foil.

3. Prepare the stuffing. Slice the fennel finely, then divide between the fish cavities. Add the tomato, olives, parsley and garlic. Add a couple of slices of lemon to each fish cavity and season with salt and pepper, before pouring the cider or water over the fish equally. Lay 2 slices of lemon on top of each fish. Lightly spray both fish with a little oil. Draw up the foil to make 2 loosely sealed parcels.

4. Transfer to the air fryer basket, spaced apart, and air-fry for 12–15 minutes.

5. Carefully remove from the basket, unwrap the parcels and serve with a salad, made with the remainder of the fennel, some young spinach leaves, diced tomatoes, a few green olives and a handful of basil leaves. Toss in a vinaigrette.

FIVE SPICE CHICKEN WITH ONIONS AND PEPPERS

This delicious chicken dish uses very little oil and is quick to cook yet full of flavour. The vegetables are cooked with the chicken so all you need to prepare is some rice to accompany the dish, and maybe a side salad.

Serves 4

Ingredients

4 skinless chicken thigh fillets

1 orange or red pepper, deseeded and sliced

2 medium red onions, sliced

1 tbsp olive oil

2 tsp runny honey

1 tbsp Chinese 5 spice

1 tsp dried parsley

1 tsp garam masala

Salt

Rice or salad, to serve

1. Put the chicken thighs and vegetables into a large mixing bowl.

2. Prepare the marinade. In a small bowl, combine the oil with the honey, Chinese 5 spice, parsley, garam masala and some salt. Stir well, then pour over the chicken and vegetables. Stir well to coat. Cover the bowl and set aside for 15 minutes, or chill overnight, if preferred.

3. When ready to cook, remove the bowl from the fridge and leave at room temperature for 15 minutes before cooking.

4. Heat the air fryer to 190°C.

5. Using tongs, transfer the chicken to the basket of the air fryer. Air-fry for 7 minutes before turning each piece of chicken over.

6. Add the vegetables to the chicken in the basket with any remaining marinade. Air-fry for 8–12 minutes, until the chicken is cooked through and the veg are golden.

7. Serve the chicken and vegetables with the delicious cooking juices collected in the base of air fryer basket poured over, along with some rice or a salad.

FILLET STEAK WITH PORTOBELLO MUSHROOMS AND RED WINE JUS

Fillet steak is deliciously tender when cooked in the air fryer. Timings may vary slightly according to the type and size of air fryer. You are the one in charge of how you prefer your steak to be cooked, and you will soon get used to this new way of cooking it. Using these timings, the steak will be cooked about medium. For rare, allow just 3 minutes on each side. Serve with the jus, the potato wedges on p153 and a tossed green salad.

Serves 2

Ingredients

2 fillet steaks (about 140g each), at room temperature
Pinch of garlic granules (optional)
25g softened butter
Oil spray
2 medium Portobello mushrooms, thickly sliced
Salt and ground black pepper
Tossed green salad, to serve
Coriander, freshly chopped, to serve

For the red wine jus

1 tbsp olive oil
½ medium red onion, finely chopped
1 small celery stick, finely chopped
75ml port
75ml red wine
1 bay leaf
300ml beef stock
1 tsp tomato ketchup
1 tsp runny honey

1. Heat the air fryer to 200°C.

2. Blot the steaks dry between sheets of absorbent kitchen paper. Season with a little salt and pepper and the garlic granules, if using. Spread one side of each steak with the butter and lightly spray the basket with a little oil. Put the prepared steaks, side by side but not touching, into the air fryer basket. Air-fry for 3 minutes.

3. Flip over the steaks and add the mushrooms, sprayed on both sides with 6 sprays of oil. Air-fry for a further 3–4 minutes, or until the steak is cooked to your liking. Remove and rest the steaks for a further 5 minutes to allow the meat to tenderise.

4. Meanwhile, make the jus. Heat the oil in a medium saucepan over a medium heat. Add the onion and celery and fry, stirring now and again, for 10 minutes, until soft and lightly golden. Pour in the port and wine and add the bay leaf. Bubble away fast, for 10 minutes, until the liquid has reduced by half. Stir in the stock, tomato ketchup and honey. Return to the boil and bubble away for a further 5–7 minutes, until reduced by half again and slightly thickened. Keep warm on the hob.

5. When the steak is ready to serve, add any cooking juices left in the base of drawer to the jus. If preferred, pass the jus through a sieve into a warm gravy jug. Discard the onion, celery and bay leaf.

6. Serve with the red wine jus, potato wedges and salad.

FESTIVE SALMON SIDE WITH DILL SAUCE

This is an attractive, popular dish and is great for a celebration family lunch. The cooked salmon is delicious hot or cold.

Ingredients

500g side of salmon, skin on and any pin bones removed

Juice of 1 satsuma

1 satsuma unpeeled and sliced

1 red chilli, deseeded and chopped, or ½ tsp chopped chillies, from a jar

2 tbsp soy sauce

1 tbsp maple syrup

1 tbsp chopped fresh parsley or coriander

Oil spray

15g butter, shaved

For the dill sauce

4 tbsp crème fraîche

2 tbsp natural Greek yoghurt

1 tsp Dijon mustard

1 tsp tomato ketchup

Zest of ½ lemon and 1 tbsp juice

2 tbsp chopped fresh dill

Salt and ground black pepper

1. Blot the salmon dry between sheets of absorbent kitchen paper. Arrange the salmon in a single layer in a shallow dish, skin side down.

2. In a mug, combine the satsuma juice with the chillies, soy sauce and maple syrup. Stir in the parsley. Pour this over the fish and set aside for 10–15 minutes to allow the flavours to mingle.

3. Heat the air fryer to 190°C. Lightly spray the air fryer basket with a little oil.

4. Carefully lift the salmon into the basket, skin side down. Add the sliced satsuma and the butter shavings, arranged evenly spaced along the length of salmon. Air-fry for 14–16 minutes, until the fish is cooked to your liking.

5. Meanwhile, make the sauce. In a medium mixing bowl, combine all the ingredients for the sauce. Stir well and turn into a serving dish.

6. Transfer the cooked salmon to a serving platter and serve garnished with the freshly chopped parsley or coriander. Serve with the sauce.

SNACKS
AND SIDES

FRENCH FRIES

The air fryer is brilliant at cooking both frozen chips and homemade French fries. I use either Maris Piper or King Edward potatoes when I make this recipe. Our grandchildren love the flavour of my homemade fries, cooked in only 1 tablespoon of oil.

Serves 2

Ingredients

2 large white baking potatoes
1 tbsp sunflower oil
1 tsp semolina or polenta
Salt

1. Peel the potatoes, if preferred, but they are best left unpeeled for extra nutrients. Cut into thick slices, along the longer length of the potato. Cut the slices into fries. Put the fries into a mixing bowl and cover with cold water. Set aside for 20 minutes. This soaking is not strictly necessary, but it does get rid of some of the excess starch, so helping the fries to crisp up nicely.

2. Drain the potatoes well, then blot dry using either a clean tea towel or sheets of absorbent kitchen paper.

3. Heat the air fryer to 190°C.

4. Turn the fries into a clean, dry mixing bowl. Add the semolina or polenta and a seasoning of salt. Add oil and mix well.

5. Turn the fries into the air fryer basket. Air-fry for 15–18 minutes, until crisp and golden, shaking after 10 minutes.

6. Shake and serve, sprinkled with salt.

ROAST MIXED NUTS

Roast nuts keep well in a sealed jar for up to 4 days. They are great sprinkled over many vegetable dishes, including coleslaw. Delicious served with cereal at breakfast time, too.

Serves 4–6

Accessories

Baking tin, approx.
  18cm square x 8cm deep, or
  a similar size solid cake tin or
  soufflé dish

Ingredients

350g packet mixed nuts, such as
  hazelnuts, almonds, walnuts,
  pistachios and Brazil nuts
Oil spray
½ tsp ground cinnamon
¼ tsp smoked sweet paprika
¼ tsp ground ginger
2.5g sesame seeds
Salt (optional)

1. Heat the air fryer to 180°C.

2. Roughly chop any larger nuts, then arrange the nuts in the tin. Lightly spray with a little oil. Sprinkle over the cinnamon, paprika and ginger and stir well.

3. Transfer the tin to the air fryer basket. Air-fry for 9 minutes, stirring twice during cooking, after 3 and 6 minutes. Sprinkle over the sesame seeds and continue to air-fry for 1 minute.

4. Remove the basket from the machine and leave the nuts in the container until cool enough to handle. Season with a little salt, if using.

5. Store in a cool place, in an airtight container.

> ### TIP:
> For a delicious sweet version, stir
> 1 tablespoon of maple syrup into the nuts
> with the oil and spices. Air-fry for
> 7–9 minutes, stirring frequently.

BAKED HALLOUMI CHEESE WITH HERBS AND GARLIC DIP

Halloumi cheese is often known as squeaky cheese because it makes your teeth squeak when you eat it. This speedily cooked halloumi makes a healthy snack with the garlic dip – you can also serve the dip with celery and carrot sticks on the side.

Serves 4

Ingredients

225g block halloumi cheese
1–2 tsp olive oil
½ tsp dried mixed herbs
Oil spray

For the garlic dip

1 tsp tomato ketchup
1 tsp lemon juice
100ml soured cream or crème
   fraíche
1 garlic clove, crushed
Salt and ground black pepper

1. Heat the air fryer to 190°C.

2. Remove the halloumi from the fridge. Unwrap, blot dry with absorbent kitchen paper and cut into 6 equal slices. Arrange on a chopping board and brush all over with the olive oil. Sprinkle with the herbs.

3. Arrange the halloumi in the lightly oiled basket, ensuring the pieces of cheese are not touching.
   Air-fry for about 6 minutes, flipping the cheese after 4 minutes, or until golden.

4. To make the dip, put all ingredients into a medium bowl, then stir to blend. Transfer to a bowl and serve with the cooked halloumi.

> ## TIP:
> Use vegetarian-friendly cheese if you are serving vegetarians.

SCOTCH EGGS

This British picnic favourite cooks brilliantly in the air fryer. As the resulting Scotch eggs are large, one half per person is often plenty. If, like me, you are not keen on the traditional breadcrumb coating, the eggs work just as well wrapped only in sausage meat – just coat with about 4 sprays of oil, per egg, before cooking, and cook them naked. The timings remain the same.

Makes 2 Scotch eggs

Ingredients

2 large eggs, plus 1 small beaten egg

2 sprigs of fresh thyme, leaves only, or ½ tsp dried thyme

300g pork sausage meat

1½ tbsp plain flour

4 tbsp panko breadcrumbs

Oil spray

Cooked asparagus or a mixed salad, to serve

Salt and ground black pepper

TIP:
Use one hand only while coating the eggs, that way you have one clean hand free, which is useful if the phone rings!

1. Heat the air fryer to 120°C if hard-boiling the eggs in the machine; heat to 180°C to cook the prepared Scotch eggs.

2. Either hard-boil the eggs in a pan of boiling water on the hob for 7 minutes, or air-fry them in the air fryer basket at 120°C for 13 minutes. In both cases, plunge the cooked eggs immediately into a bowl of ice-cold water. Set aside until cold, then peel the eggs, very carefully, under the water. Blot the eggs dry with absorbent kitchen paper.

3. Massage the thyme leaves and a light seasoning of salt and pepper into the sausage meat, then divide into 2 even-size portions. Using a little flour and a rolling pin, roll both pieces of sausage meat into a square, approximately 14cm x 14cm.

4. Wrap each egg completely in a piece of sausage meat, making 2 oval balls.

5. Put the remaining flour into one bowl, the beaten egg into a second bowl and the breadcrumbs into a third bowl. Coat each prepared Scotch egg in the flour first, then the beaten egg, and lastly the breadcrumbs. Spray very lightly with a little oil.

6. Transfer to the air fryer basket and air-fry at 180°C for 16–18 minutes, flipping over after 7 minutes.

7. Serve immediately with cooked asparagus or a tossed mixed salad.

CRISPY CHICKEN WITH PARMESAN

A great alternative to fish fingers. Serve with salad and the Salsa on page 59.

Serves 2

Ingredients

325g chicken breast mini
    fillets or 2 small chicken
    breast fillets, cut into
    fingers
1 medium size egg
4 tbsp plain flour
4 tbsp panko breadcrumbs
1 tsp fajita seasoning
30g Parmesan cheese,
    finely grated
Oil spray
Salt and ground black pepper

To serve

Mixed salad
Salsa (see page 59)

1. Blot the chicken strips dry between sheets of absorbent kitchen paper.

2. In a shallow, wide cereal or soup bowl, beat the egg. In a second similar bowl, combine the flour and breadcrumbs with the fajita seasoning, a little salt and pepper and the Parmesan cheese.

3. Working in 2 batches, dip the chicken into the beaten egg and then into the breadcrumb mixture to coat on all sides. Transfer to a large plate and continue with the remaining chicken. Chill for 15 minutes.

4. Heat the air fryer to 200°C. Spray the basket with a little oil, then spray the tops of each prepared chicken piece with a little oil.

5. Arrange the chicken in the air fryer basket, not quite touching, and in a single layer.

6. Air-fry for approximately 10 minutes, turning each piece after 6 minutes. The chicken is ready when it is crisp, golden, cooked through and smelling delicious!

7. Serve with a salad and the Salsa.

SKINNY SWEET POTATO FRIES WITH TOMATO DIP

These fries are every bit as tasty as the conventionally fried version, but better for you, due to the reduced amount of added fat. They are delicious with poultry and fish dishes, or just on their own, served with the tomato dip. Not peeling the potatoes gives you an extra hit of fibre and vitamins.

Serves 2

Ingredients

2 large sweet potatoes
1 tsp fine semolina or cornflour
    (optional, but helps to crisp
    potatoes)
2 tsp sweet paprika
2 tbsp rapeseed or sunflower oil
Oil spray
Salt and ground black pepper

For the tomato dip

3 rounded tbsp natural Greek
    yoghurt
2 tsp tomato ketchup
1–2 tsp lemon juice, to taste
½ tsp chopped chillies, from a jar

1. Heat the air fryer to 200°C.

2. Slice the potatoes into long slices, then cut into shoe-string fries. Blot dry with absorbent kitchen paper. Place the fries into a medium mixing bowl, then add the semolina or cornflour, if using, with the paprika and some salt and pepper. Add the rapeseed or sunflower oil and toss to coat.

3. Cook in 2 batches. Lightly spray the air fryer basket with oil. Put the first batch into the basket and air-fry for 8–12 minutes, until crispy, removing the basket and shaking after 5 minutes. Repeat with the second batch.

4. Meanwhile, make the tomato dip. Put all the ingredients into a medium mixing bowl and stir to combine. Turn into a serving dish and chill until ready to serve.

5. If necessary, add the first batch of fries to the second batch at the end of cooking, shake to combine, then continue to air-fry for 2–3 minutes, until piping hot.

6. Shake and serve with the tomato dip.

ROAST HERBY TOMATOES

Tomatoes are quick and easy to air-fry with the addition of very little fat. Serve for breakfast with wholemeal toast and mashed avocado, or as a side dish at any time.

Serves 4

Ingredients

4 medium tomatoes, cut in
   half horizontally
1 tsp dried mixed herbs
25g butter or 1 tbsp olive oil
Salt and ground black pepper

1. Heat the air fryer to 190°C.

2. Arrange the tomato halves, cut side up, in the base of the air fryer basket. Season with a little salt and pepper. Scatter the herbs evenly over the tomatoes.

3. Top each half tomato with a tiny amount of the butter, or brush with a little olive oil.

4. Air-fry for 10–12 minutes, until cooked to your liking.

5. Serve immediately.

SAUTÉ POTATOES WITH CREAMY DIPPING SAUCE

These speedy crispy potatoes are very like potato crisps, as we know them. Good served as a snack or side dish at any time of the day. Cook in 2 batches for crisp results and they are delicious with or without the dip. Serve the potatoes hot, seasoned with salt.

Serves 2

Ingredients

2 large white baking potatoes, peeled (I like Maris Piper or King Edward)
1 medium sweet potato, peeled
Juice of ½ lemon
Oil spray

For the yoghurt dipping sauce (optional)

4 tbsp crème fraîche
2 tbsp natural Greek yoghurt
2 tsp lemon juice
2 tsp tomato ketchup
1 tsp wholegrain mustard
Salt and ground black pepper

TIP:
Soaking the potatoes is not strictly necessary, but it does get rid of some of the starch, which helps the potatoes to crisp.

1. Slice the potatoes thinly using a sharp knife, then transfer to a large bowl of salted water, ensuring the potatoes are well covered. Add the lemon juice. Cover and set aside for 30 minutes or up to 7 hours. No time to do this? Simply rinse the potato slices well in cold water.

2. Heat the air fryer to 190°C.

3. Drain and rinse the potatoes, then blot the slices dry, either between sheets of absorbent kitchen paper or rolled up in a clean tea towel. It is important that they are as dry as possible before air-frying, so they crisp up well.

4. Put the dried potato slices into a large mixing bowl. Spray the potato slices evenly with about 8 sprays of oil, tossing as you go so that each side is evenly coated.

5. Transfer half of the potato slices to the air fryer basket, well spaced out.

6. Air-fry for 10–12 minutes. Shake the basket, or stir the potatoes to re-distribute, twice during cooking.

7. Turn this first batch into a serving dish and set aside. Repeat with the remaining potato slices, air-frying as before.

8. Finally, return the first batch to the air fryer, on top of the second batch. Toss lightly or stir together gently. Air-fry for 2–3 minutes until crisp and golden.

9. If making the dip, put all the dip ingredients into a medium mixing bowl. Add a light seasoning of salt and pepper, then stir well to combine.

ADAM'S SOUTH AFRICAN BILTONG

My youngest son gave me this delicious recipe. It's an ideal snack for those on low-carb diets and is very popular with students. Once cool, store the biltong in a Kilner jar, lined with absorbent kitchen paper. However, biltong is so popular it will not be there for long!

Serves 4

Accessories (optional)
Liner

Ingredients
2 x 180g rump steaks
2 tbsp beef dry rub or biltong spice
   rub (available from specialist
   shops and online)
Oil spray

1. Remove the fat from the steaks and discard, then bash out the meat a little, using a steak hammer or a rolling pin.

2. Place the prepared meat into a mixing bowl and add the meat rub. Stir to coat the steaks evenly, then cover and chill for 5 hours or overnight.

3. Heat the air fryer to 100°C.

4. Lightly spray the meat with a little oil. Using a lightly oiled liner, if available, turn the meat into the air fryer basket. Air-fry for 1¼ hours, until dried. Turn the meat 3 times during cooking, after 20, 30 and 40 minutes.

5. Remove from the air fryer, transfer to a dish, and allow to cool. Cut into very thin slices to serve.

> ### TIP:
> For economy, you could use beef skirt instead of rump steak – useful for students to know!

PARMESAN POTATO WEDGES WITH CHICKPEA AND SUN-DRIED TOMATO DIP

These crisp potato wedges are cooked in the air fryer in less than 20 minutes. Delicious with the tasty hummus-style chickpea and sun-dried tomato dip, or just on their own as a snack. The dip can also be served with carrot, celery and red pepper sticks.

Serves 2

Ingredients

2 medium white baking potatoes, unpeeled, cut into wedges. (I like Maris Piper or King Edward) potatoes

1 tbsp sunflower oil or rapeseed oil

1 tsp sweet paprika

½ tsp salt

50g Parmesan cheese, grated

For the chickpea and sun-dried tomato dip

410g tin chickpeas, drained and rinsed

100g sun-dried tomatoes, drained weight, roughly chopped

4 tbsp of olive oil from the sun-dried tomatoes

Small handful of chopped fresh coriander or parsley

½ garlic clove, chopped, or ½ tsp chopped garlic, from a jar

¼ tsp chopped chillies, from a jar

1 tsp lemon juice

Approx. 8 tbsp cold water

Salt and ground black pepper

1. Heat the air fryer to 190°C.

2. Blot the potato wedges dry between sheets of absorbent kitchen paper. Put the wedges into a medium mixing bowl, then add the oil with the paprika, salt and Parmesan cheese. Toss to coat well.

3. Transfer the wedges to the air fryer basket, in a single layer, if possible. Air-fry for 13 minutes, until crisp and golden, removing the basket and shaking or turning the wedges over using a fish slice after 8 minutes.

4. Meanwhile, put all the dip ingredients into a food processor. Blend to a smooth purée, adding the water, little by little, until the preferred consistency is reached.

5. Serve the dip in a small dish alongside the potato wedges.

HASSELBACK POTATOES WITH BLUE CHEESE DIP

These potatoes are so speedy to prepare and cook. I often serve them without the dip, as a side with the Sunday roast. Use a mixture of red and white potatoes for a splash of colour.

Serves 4

Ingredients

8–10 medium potatoes, each about the size of a large hen's egg
1–2 tsp olive oil
Salt and ground black pepper
Small handful of rosemary, chopped

For the blue cheese dip (optional)

50g blue cheese, such as Stilton, roughly chopped
30ml mayonnaise
100g natural Greek yoghurt
1 tsp lemon juice

1. Heat the air fryer to 190°C.

2. Put the potatoes onto a chopping board and cut slits all along the top of each potato, making sure you do not cut right through to the bottom. Brush them with the oil and sprinkle with salt and pepper.

3. Lay, not touching, in the air fryer basket. Air-fry for 20–25 minutes, shaking the basket or turning the potatoes over twice during cooking – after 10 and 17 minutes. The potatoes will have golden crisp skins and soft fluffy interiors.

4. Meanwhile, make the dip, if using. Put all the ingredients into a food processor and process until smooth. Transfer to serving bowl and chill until ready to serve.

5. Sprinkle the hot potatoes with salt and chopped rosemary and serve with the creamy dip.

> **TIP:**
> Use vegetarian-friendly cheese if serving vegetarians.

ROASTED VEGETABLE MEDLEY

Full of flavour and easy to cook all together, this colourful roasted vegetable dish is delicious served with a Sunday roast.

Serves 4

Ingredients

3 carrots, sliced diagonally

1 medium sweet potato, cut into cubes

½ small butternut squash, peeled and cut into cubes

1 red pepper, deseeded and sliced

1 tbsp sunflower oil

1 tsp dried parsley

Salt and ground black pepper

1. Heat the air fryer to 190°C.

2. Put the prepared vegetables into a medium mixing bowl and add the sunflower oil, parsley and a good seasoning of salt and pepper. Toss together.

3. Tip the prepared vegetables into the air fryer basket and air-fry for 14–17 minutes, or until vegetables are tender, shaking the basket after 8 minutes.

4. Shake and serve immediately.

ROASTED CARROTS AND PARSNIPS

Add a bit of variety by coating the oiled vegetables with a tablespoon of grated Parmesan cheese, mixed with a teaspoon of semolina, for extra crunch, before air-frying.

Serves 2

Ingredients
200g parsnips, cut into sticks
300g carrots, cut into sticks
Oil spray or 1 tbsp olive oil
1½ tsp garam masala (optional)
Salt and ground black pepper

1. Heat the air fryer to 180°C.

2. Put the prepared vegetables into a medium mixing bowl. Spray with a little oil or toss in olive oil. Sprinkle with the garam masala, if using, a little salt and plenty of pepper. Toss again.

3. Transfer the vegetables to the air fryer basket. Air-fry for 15–18 minutes, shaking the basket or turning the vegetables a couple of times during cooking, after 5 and 9 minutes, to ensure even browning.

ROAST MUSHROOMS AND COLOURFUL PEPPERS

This speedy to cook, attractive vegetable dish is packed full of fibre. A good accompaniment to mid-week meals.

Serves 2

Ingredients
200g button mushrooms, sliced
2 orange or red peppers, deseeded
   and roughly chopped
Oil spray or 1 tbsp olive oil
1 tsp dried mixed herbs
Salt and ground black pepper

1. Heat the air fryer to 190°C.

2. Place the prepared vegetables in a mixing bowl. Lightly spray all over with a little oil or toss in olive oil.

3. Sprinkle with the mixed herbs, some salt and pepper and toss to coat. Place in the air fryer basket and air-fry for 5–8 minutes.

4. Remove the air fryer basket and shake or turn the vegetables gently. Air-fry at 200°C for 2 minutes until golden.

5. Shake and serve.

PUDDINGS
AND CAKES

SPEEDY CARROT CAKE MUFFINS

These easy to make carrot cake muffins can be cooked together if using an air fryer rack. If not, cook the cakes in 2 batches, spaced slightly apart on the base of your air fryer basket. The cooking time will be about the same. These delicious muffins will keep in an airtight container in a cool place for up to 3 days or will freeze well for up to 3 months.

Makes 12 muffins

Accessories

12 small silicone cake cases or
   24 paper fairy cake cases
   (doubled up for extra support)
Metal rack (optional)

Ingredients

150g self-raising flour
150g wholemeal flour
1 level tsp baking powder
½ tsp ground cinnamon (optional)
75g soft light brown sugar
100g carrots, grated
50g pecan nuts or walnuts,
   chopped
2 large eggs
125ml sunflower or rapeseed oil
1–2 tbsp semi-skimmed milk
1 tbsp sunflower seeds (optional,
   but nice)
1 tsp sifted icing sugar (optional),
   to serve

1. Heat the air fryer to 170°C.

2. In a large mixing bowl, combine the flours, baking powder, cinnamon, if using, and the brown sugar. Add the carrots and stir roughly to combine. Stir in the nuts.

3. In a medium mixing bowl, combine the eggs, oil and a tablespoon of the milk. Beat well with a fork.

4. Make a well in the centre of the flour and carrot mixture and pour in the oil and eggs. Using a wooden spoon, beat well to form a batter, adding the extra tablespoon of milk if necessary. Don't over beat, you need a soft dropping consistency, with no visible sign of the flour.

5. Using a dessert spoon and a teaspoon, divide the mixture evenly between the cake cases. Top each muffin with a few of the sunflower seeds, if using.

6. If using the rack, arrange 6 muffins in the base of the air fryer, making sure they are not quite touching. Add the rack and arrange the remaining cakes on top, spaced evenly. Air-fry for 10–11 minutes, until well risen and golden brown. If you don't have a metal rack, cook in 2 batches.

7. Carefully remove from the air fryer and cool on a wire cooling rack.

8. Serve sprinkled with sifted icing sugar if you like.

APPLE, PEAR AND RASPBERRY CRUMBLE

I first made this fruity crumble using windfalls from the garden, then added raspberries for a certain richness and wonderful flavour. I have used less sugar here than in usual crumble recipes, for a healthier pudding.

Serves 4

Accessories
Baking tin with handle or non-stick, solid-base cake tin (approx. 18cm square x 8cm deep)
Foil sling (see page 18)

Ingredients
2 cooking apples (I like Bramley), peeled, cored and sliced
1 just-ripe pear (I like Conference pears), peeled, cored and sliced
125g raspberries or blackberries, defrosted if frozen
75g demerara sugar
1 tbsp granulated sweetener
Cream or crème fraîche, to serve

For the crumble topping
150g plain flour
25g porridge oats
100g chilled butter, cut into cubes
75g demerara sugar
1 tbsp granulated sweetener
1 tbsp ground almonds
1 tbsp flaked toasted almonds
1 tbsp pumpkin seeds

1. Heat the air fryer to 180°C.

2. Place the apples and pears in the baking tin. Add the raspberries or blackberries with the sugar and sweetener. Stir gently. Cover with a piece of foil, place in the air fryer basket and air-fry for 8–10 minutes. Remove from the air fryer and take off the foil. Stir gently.

3. While the fruit is cooking, make the topping. In a large mixing bowl, put the flour, oats and butter. Rub in the butter until the mixture resembles breadcrumbs.

4. Stir in the sugar, sweetener, ground almonds, flaked almonds and the pumpkin seeds. Tip the crumble over the par-cooked fruit. Press down lightly.

5. Return the tin to the air fryer basket, uncovered, and air-fry at 180°C for 20–25 minutes, until the fruit is soft, and the crumble is cooked and lightly golden. Check after 15 minutes, and cover with foil if the topping is becoming too brown.

6. Serve warm, with cream or crème fraîche.

> ### TIP:
> Those with large air fryers may like to use 1½ times the ingredients, to serve 6 people. Cook the revised crumble in a larger dish, increasing cooking time by about 5–7 minutes.

BANANA BREAD

While on holiday in Jamaica recently, we had delicious freshly baked banana bread each morning for breakfast. I returned home determined to develop a recipe for my air fryer, and here it is.

Accessories

Baking tin with handle or non-stick, solid-base cake tin (approx. 18cm square x 8cm deep, greased with a little softened butter)

Foil sling (see page 18)

Ingredients

4 ripe small bananas or 3 large bananas

60g softened butter, plus extra for serving (optional)

70g soft light brown sugar

3 tbsp black treacle

2 large eggs, beaten

200g self-raising flour

1 tsp ground ginger

½ tsp ground nutmeg

½ tsp ground cloves

Icing sugar, to serve

1. Heat the air fryer to 160°C.

2. Peel and slice all but half a banana into a large mixing bowl. Add the butter, sugar and treacle. Mash with a fork until puréed. Using a wooden spoon, beat in the eggs.

3. In a separate mixing bowl, combine the flour and spices. Add the dry ingredients to the banana mixture. Beat with a wooden spoon, to form a soft batter.

4. Pour the batter into the prepared tin and level the surface. Top with the remaining half a banana, sliced.

5. Place in the air fryer basket and air-fry for 25–30 minutes, until risen and a wooden cocktail stick inserted into the centre comes out clean. Remove from the air fryer.

6. Allow to stand in the tin for 10 minutes, then turn out and cool completely on a wire cooling rack.

7. Dust with sifted icing sugar and serve in small slices, spread with a little softened butter, if preferred.

PINEAPPLE AND CHOCOLATE PUDDING

You can use any kind of pineapple for this recipe – fresh, frozen or tinned – but whatever your choice, blot the pineapple dry between several sheets of absorbent kitchen paper before using. Serve the pudding hot or warm with piping-hot custard.

Serves 8

Accessories
Baking tin or non-stick, solid-base cake tin (approx. 18cm square by 8cm deep), greased with a little softened butter

Ingredients
200g self-raising flour, plus extra for dusting
2 tbsp cocoa powder, sifted
100g chilled butter, cut into cubes,
80g soft brown sugar
2 rounded tbsp granulated sweetener
3 large eggs, beaten
3 tbsp semi-skimmed milk
225g fresh, frozen and defrosted, or tinned in fruit juice pineapple slices (drained, if using canned pineapple), blotted dry and roughly chopped
Custard, to serve

1. Heat the air fryer to 170°C.

2. Add about half a tablespoon of flour to the greased tin and shake and tilt until the base and sides are coated with a little flour. Discard any surplus flour.

3. Put the flour and cocoa powder into a large mixing bowl. Using your fingertips, rub in the chilled butter until the mixture resembles breadcrumbs. Stir in the sugar and the sweetener.

4. Beat the eggs and milk together in a jug, then pour into the flour mixture. Beat, using a wooden spoon, for about 30 seconds to form a soft batter.

5. Fold the prepared pineapple into the batter, then pour into the prepared tin and level the surface. Carefully place the tin into the air fryer basket. Air-fry for 25–30 minutes, until well risen and springy to the touch. A metal skewer or wooden cocktail stick inserted into the centre should come out clean.

6. Remove from the air fryer and allow to stand for 15 minutes before turning out onto a serving platter.

7. Serve the warm pudding in small slices with hot custard.

FRUITY YORKSHIRE PUDDINGS

This recipe can be used as a great accompaniment to the Sunday roast, and, also, to make this delicious dessert. For ease and speed, snip the drained apricots into small pieces, using kitchen scissors.

Serves 4

Accessories

4 x 9cm ramekins, 6cm high, or 4 x large silicone muffin cases, (or you could use empty, clean, 112g tuna fish tins!), lightly greased.

Ingredients

400g tin apricots in natural juice, drained

About 12 small strawberries, halved

4 tsp sunflower oil

For the batter

60g plain flour

¼ tsp salt

2 large eggs, beaten

175ml whole or semi-skimmed milk

To serve

Sifted icing sugar (optional)

Single cream or crème fraîche

1. Make the batter. Put the flour and salt into a medium mixing bowl. Make a dent in the centre and pour in the beaten eggs with half the milk. Using a wooden spoon, beat gently to form a smooth batter. Add the remaining milk and continue to beat for 5 minutes, using a balloon whisk. Transfer to a jug. The batter improves if it is set aside for 15 minutes or covered and chilled for up to 3 hours, or overnight.

2. Heat the air fryer to 200°C.

3. Arrange the ramekins in the air fryer basket. Add 1 teaspoon of oil to each prepared ramekin. Slot the basket into the machine and air-fry for 5 minutes, until smoking hot. Stir the batter again, then carefully pour it into the 4 ramekins, dividing it evenly between them. Air-fry for about 11 minutes, until well risen and golden. Do not open the fryer until 10 minutes have passed.

4. Meanwhile, roughly chop the drained apricots and put into a medium mixing bowl. Add strawberries and muddle together.

5. Serve the Yorkshire puddings immediately, topped with the fruit, sprinkled with a little sifted icing sugar, if using, and some single cream or crème fraîche.

ROASTED PEACHES OR NECTARINES, WITH GINGER

The combination of the fruit with brown sugar, honey and ginger is comforting and warming as well as tasting good. A delicious autumn dessert.

Serves 2

Accessories
Baking tin with handle or non-stick, solid-base cake tin (approx. 18cm square by 8cm deep)

Ingredients
2 large ripe peaches or nectarines, halved and stoned
½ thumb-sized piece of fresh ginger, peeled and grated
1 rounded tbsp soft light brown sugar
1 tbsp runny honey
½ tsp ground cinnamon
Juice of 1 lime or lemon
Toasted flaked almonds and crème fraîche, to serve

1. Put the prepared peaches or nectarines, hollow side up, into the tin in a single layer.

2. In a small mixing bowl, combine the ginger, sugar, honey, cinnamon and the lime or lemon juice. Stir, then divide the mixture between the hollows of the 4 peach halves, pouring any extra juice over the fruit. Set aside for 15 minutes to allow the flavours to mingle.

3. Heat the air fryer to 180°C.

4. Place the container into the air fryer basket and air-fry for 7–10 minutes, until the peaches are soft – the cooking time will vary according to the ripeness of the fruit.

5. Delicious served hot or warm, with a sprinkling of toasted flaked almonds and a dollop of crème fraîche.

> ## TIP:
> To peel ginger easily, scrape the skin off using the edge of a metal teaspoon.

CHEESE SCONES

These light and fluffy scones are super quick to cook in the air fryer. The mustard and cayenne pepper really bring out the flavour of the cheese. Light and delicious, you can serve these straight from the machine, for lunch or at tea-time, spread with a little soft butter.

Makes 6 scones

Accessories
6cm scone cutter

Ingredients
175g self-raising flour, plus extra
    for dusting
½ tsp baking powder
Pinch of cayenne pepper
½ tsp mustard powder
Pinch of salt
50g butter, cubed and chilled
50g hard cheese, such as mature
    Cheddar, grated
25g Parmesan cheese, grated
1 large egg
75ml semi-skimmed milk
Oil spray

1. Heat the air fryer to 190°C.

2. In a large mixing bowl, combine the flour, baking powder, cayenne pepper, mustard powder and salt. Using your fingertips, rub the butter into the flour until the mixture resembles breadcrumbs. Stir in all the cheese.

3. Beat the egg and milk together in a jug. Reserve just enough of the milk and egg mixture to brush over the top of the scones before baking. Using a table knife, stir the remaining mixture into the dry ingredients to form a soft dough. You need a slightly wetter dough than when making scones to be cooked in a conventional oven.

4. Tip out the dough onto a lightly floured board, then roll out to a thickness of about 18mm. Cut out 6 thick scones using a floured cutter, re-rolling the dough if necessary.

5. Lightly oil the air fryer basket. Arrange the scones, not touching, in the air fryer basket. Brush the tops with a little of the remaining milk mixture. Air-fry for 10–11 minutes, until well risen and golden. Remove from the air fryer. Best served warm.

For a sweet version, follow the recipe but omit the cheese, cayenne pepper and mustard and add 50g raisins and 50g caster sugar to the rubbed-in ingredients instead. The cooking time remains the same.

BAKED PEACH AND NECTARINE FILO TARTS

The cream cheese topping is optional, so if preferred, serve the fruit tarts topped with a little crème fraîche!

Serves 2

Accessories

Baking tin with handle or non-stick, solid-base cake tin (approx. 18cm square by 8cm deep)

2 individual pie dishes or ramekins

Ingredients

2 ripe peaches, halved, stoned and thickly sliced

1 ripe nectarine, halved, stoned and thickly sliced

1 tbsp runny honey

25g butter, melted

3 sheets filo pastry 34cm x 34cm, each cut into 4 equal squares

For the cream cheese topping

2 rounded tbsp cream cheese

½ tsp grated nutmeg

1 tsp granulated sweetener or 2 tsp caster sugar

To serve (optional)

50g pecan nuts, toasted and chopped

20g pumpkin seeds, toasted

1. Heat the air fryer to 170°C.

2. Arrange the peaches and the nectarine slices in a single layer, if possible, in the tin. Drizzle over the honey and place the tin in the air fryer basket. Air-fry for 6–9 minutes, or until the fruit is soft and the honey is starting to caramelise. Remove from the air fryer and set aside.

3. Put the butter in a ramekin in the air fryer at 170°C for approximately 2 minutes until melted. Using a pastry brush, grease the pie dishes or ramekins with a little of the melted butter.

4. Place a square of filo in each container, pushing it into the base and sides. Brush with the melted butter. Add another layer of filo. Brush again with butter and continue until all the filo is used up.

5. Heat the air fryer to 180°C.

6. Put the ramekins, not touching, into the air fryer basket and air-fry for about 6 minutes, until the nests are crisp and golden. Remove from the air fryer basket and set aside.

7. When ready to serve, prepare the cream cheese topping. Put the cream cheese into a mixing bowl and, using a wooden spoon, beat in the nutmeg and the sweetener. Don't over beat, or the cream cheese will go runny.

8. Divide the fruit between the cooked filo nests and serve, accompanied by a dollop of the whipped cream cheese, topped with the nuts and seeds, if using.

CHOCOLATE FONDANTS WITH RASPBERRY COULIS

This dessert is very rich and simply delicious. The fondants have a crisp crust while maintaining a gooey centre – just don't overcook them, or they will lose their molten insides. Serve the fondants straight from the oven so guests see the 'wow' factor of the liquid centres!

Serves 4

Accessories

4 very small dariole moulds or
   4 x 7.5cm diameter individual
   soufflé dishes

Ingredients

1 tsp caster sugar
1 rounded tbsp cocoa powder,
   sifted
50g softened butter
75g good-quality dark chocolate,
   I like Bourneville, broken into
   pieces
1 large egg and 1 large egg yolk
50g golden caster sugar
40g self-raising flour
Cream or creme fraiche, to serve

For the raspberry coulis

400g fresh or frozen raspberries
   (defrosted and well drained, if
   frozen)
1–2 tbsp sifted icing sugar, to taste

1. To make the coulis pass the raspberries through a sieve into a mixing bowl, stir in the sifted icing sugar and rest.

2. Combine the sugar and cocoa powder in a bowl. Grease the dishes well with a little of the butter, then dust with the sugar and cocoa powder to help the fondants turn out easily. Knock out and discard any excess.

3. Heat the air fryer to 160°C.

4. Put the remaining butter into a mixing bowl that can be used in the air fryer. Place in basket and air-fry for 2–3 minutes, until melted. Add the pieces of chocolate to the melted butter in the bowl and stir.

5. Return to the air fryer for 1–2 minutes. Stir to ensure the chocolate has melted completely into the butter.

6. In a separate bowl, using a hand-held electric mixer beat the egg, egg yolk and sugar together for about 5 minutes until light and creamy and when the whisk is lifted above you see a visible trail.

7. Using a metal spoon, fold in the melted chocolate and butter, then the flour. Divide evenly between the ramekins and run a clean, dry finger around the edge of each dish, to help the fondants rise evenly. Place the ramekins into the air fryer basket so they're not touching and air-fry for 7–9 minutes, until risen and a crust has formed on top.

8. Remove from the air fryer and carefully run a dinner knife around the edge of the puddings. Turn them out onto individual plates and serve.

APPLE CAKE

This recipe makes a fairly shallow cake if cooked in a cake tin. For a deeper cake, cook in a loaf pan. The apple cake can be served hot as a dessert or cold as a cake.

Serves 8

Accessories
Baking tin or non-stick, solid-base cake tin (approx. 18cm square by 8cm deep) or use a 1lb loaf tin
Foil sling (see page 18)

Ingredients
Softened butter, for greasing
125g self-raising flour
25g wholemeal flour
1 tsp ground ginger
1 tsp ground cinnamon
½ tsp baking powder
100g butter, cubed and chilled
80g light brown soft sugar
1 tbsp granulated sweetener
1 medium Bramley apple, peeled, cored and chopped
1 medium eating apple (I like Cox, Pink Lady or Worcester), peeled, cored and chopped
2 tbsp semi-skimmed milk
2 large eggs, beaten
1 rounded tsp demerara sugar
Crème fraîche or vanilla ice cream to serve

1. Heat the air fryer to 140°C. Lightly grease the base and sides of the tin with a little softened butter.

2. Mix both flours and the spices together in a large mixing bowl with the baking powder. Add the cubed cold butter and, using your fingertips, rub the butter into the flour until the mixture resembles breadcrumbs. Stir in the brown sugar, sweetener and the apples, reserving 3 slices of the eating apple to decorate the cake.

3. In a small mixing bowl, and using a fork, beat the milk and eggs together, then using a wooden spoon, stir the egg mixture into the flour mixture to form a stiff batter.

4. Turn the mixture into the prepared tin and level the surface. Arrange the reserved apple slices on top and sprinkle with demerara sugar.

5. Transfer to the air fryer basket and air-fry for 25–30 minutes, or until risen and golden and just set in the middle. Insert a clean skewer or cocktail stick into the centre; it should come out clean.

6. Remove the tin from the basket and set aside for 15 minutes. Either serve warm as a dessert or turn out onto a wire cooling rack and allow to cool completely.

7. Serve in small slices with a dollop of crème fraîche, or a scoop of vanilla ice cream.

BANANA AND BERRY MUFFINS

As these muffins are so deliciously light and popular with everyone, I see no reason to cook fewer than 8 – they will keep in an airtight container in a cool place for up to 3 days and freeze well for up to 3 months. The banana adds a little natural sweetness. You can, however, make the muffins without the banana; if so add an extra tablespoon of milk.

Makes 8 muffins

Accessories

8 small silicone muffin cases,
   or 16 paper fairy cake cases,
   doubled up for better support
Metal rack (optional)

Ingredients

150g self-raising flour
½ level tsp baking powder
75g soft light brown sugar
1 large egg
1 tsp vanilla extract
60ml sunflower or rapeseed oil
3–4 tbsp semi-skimmed milk
½ ripe medium banana, mashed
100g berries of your choice (I like
   blueberries and raspberries.
   Frozen and defrosted berries
   are fine)
40g chocolate chips

To serve (optional)

1 tsp icing sugar
Natural Greek yoghurt

1. Heat the air fryer to 170°C.

2. In a large mixing bowl, combine the flours, baking powder and brown sugar. In a medium mixing bowl, combine the egg, vanilla extract, oil and 3 tablespoons of the milk. Beat well with a fork, then add the mashed banana and continue to beat gently, just to combine.

3. Make a well in the centre of the flour mixture. Pour in the oil and egg mixture. Using a wooden spoon, beat to form a batter, adding the extra tablespoon of milk if necessary. You just need a soft dropping consistency, so don't over beat. Stir in the mixed berries. (If using frozen berries, drain on absorbent kitchen paper before adding.) Stir in three-quarters of the chocolate chips.

4. Using a dessert spoon and a teaspoon, divide the mixture evenly between the cake cases. Top each muffin with a few of the remaining chocolate chips.

5. If using a metal rack, arrange 3 muffins in the base of the air fryer, ensuring they are not quite touching. Add the rack, and arrange the remaining muffins, spaced evenly, on top. If you don't have a metal rack, space the muffins apart on the base of the basket or cook in batches if necessary. Air-fry for 10–12 minutes, until well risen, springy to the touch and golden.

6. Carefully remove from the air fryer and leave to cool on a wire cooling rack.

7. Sift over some icing sugar and serve accompanied by the natural Greek yoghurt if you like.

INDEX

ACKNOWLEDGEMENTS

A couple of years ago now, my son Adam Piper invited me round for coffee with the strange request that I come armed with some locally produced pork sausages, which I always keep ready in my freezer. While preparing our beverages, he placed the frozen bullets into his new kitchen toy. Amazingly, about 12 minutes later, he presented perfectly cooked golden sausages with their wonderful aroma, crisp skins and moist insides. They were cooked, of course, in his new air fryer. When I discovered they also tasted delicious, I was immediately sold.

That afternoon saw me ordering my very own air fryer online. Soon I became totally hooked and started to make extensive notes as I air-fried a vast range of foods from roast lamb to garlic bread, roast vegetables and carrot cake muffins. I even experimented with drying freshly picked mint from the garden. Urged on by friends and members of my local U3A, I started to run air fryer demonstrations and cookery classes, with participants constantly asking for my recipes. The time had come for me to write an air fryer cookbook.

As a home economist and cookery writer, I take pride in developing interesting, healthy recipes that, hopefully, you will want to return to time and time again. My grandchildren now love to make their own air-fried sausages and chips, and to cook cheese scones and muffins for tea. I am sure your children and grandchildren will also love learning how to cook their very own air-fried snacks and dishes.

There are so many people I would like to thank sincerely for their help, support and encouragement during my journey to complete this book, and to get it published. To Elizabeth Bond, Publishing Director at Ebury Partnerships at Penguin Random House, who commissioned my book. Thank you Elizabeth for allowing me to use my preferred photographer, David Selling, for the photos, and my favourite stylist and designer Madeline Meckiffe. They both worked tirelessly on each and every photo. Elizabeth appointed my editor, Fionn Hargreaves, who attended every day of the photo shoot, giving valuable and helpful advice in a lovely friendly manner. Thanks Fionn.

Thanks to my son Adam, both for introducing me to this incredible appliance, and for cooking the biltong and the Scotch eggs perfectly, delivering them ready to be photographed. Thanks to my son Iain, for constantly phoning to see how the book was coming along. Grateful thanks also to my sister Rosemary Holcombe who stayed over at my house and worked with me preparing the vast array of appetising food for photography. Thanks to my sister Mary-Anne Pitt and to my husband Malcolm for tasting copious new recipes. Thanks also to my good pal Sue Long, always so encouraging and supportive.

Lastly, but by no means least, thank you to you, my readers, for buying this book. With encouragement from family and friends, I am now working on my second air fryer cookery book, so watch this space!

Published in 2023 by Ebury Press,
an imprint of Ebury Publishing
20 Vauxhall Bridge Road
London SW1V 2SA

Penguin
Random House
UK

Ebury Press is part of Penguin Random House,
group of companies whose addresses can be found at
global.penguinrandomhouse.com
2

Food preparation: Beverley Jarvis and Rosemary Holcombe,
  with assistance from Adam Piper
Food styling: Madeline Meckiffe
Props styling: Faye Wears
Photographer: David-James Selling
Design: Madeline Meckiffe
Production: Serena Nazareth
Project editor: Fionn Hargreaves
Publishing director: Elizabeth Bond

Printed and bound by Mohn Media in Germany

This edition first published by Ebury Press in 2023
www.penguin.co.uk
A CIP catalogue record for this book is available
from the British Library ISBN 9781529918526